easy to make!
BBQs & Grills

Good Housekeeping

easy to make!
BBQs & Grills

COLLINS & BROWN

First published in Great Britain in 2008
by Collins & Brown
10 Southcombe Street
London W14 0RA

An imprint of Anova Books Company Ltd

The Good Housekeeping website is
www.goodhousekeeping.co.uk

1 2 3 4 5 6 7 8 9

ISBN 978-1-84340-449-1

A catalogue record for this book is available from the British
Library.

Reproduction by Dot Gradations Ltd
Printed and bound by SNP Leefung, China

This book can be ordered direct from the publisher. Contact the
marketing department, but try your bookshop first.

www.anovabooks.com

NOTES

- Both metric and imperial measures are given for the
  recipes. Follow either set of measures, not a mixture
  of both, as they are not interchangeable.
- All spoon measures are level.
  1 tsp = 5ml spoon; 1 tbsp = 15ml spoon.
- Ovens and grills must be preheated to the specified
  temperature.
- Use sea salt and freshly ground black pepper unless
  otherwise suggested.
- Fresh herbs should be used unless dried herbs are
  specified in a recipe.
- Medium eggs should be used except where
  otherwise specified. Free-range eggs are
  recommended.
- Note that certain recipes, including mayonnaise,
  lemon curd and some cold desserts, contain raw or
  lightly cooked eggs. The young, elderly, pregnant
  women and anyone with an immune-deficiency
  disease should avoid these, because of the slight risk
  of salmonella.
- Calorie, fat and carbohydrate counts per serving are
  provided for the recipes.

Picture Credits
Photographers: Nicki Dowey; Craig Robertson (all Basics
photography)
Stylist: Helen Trent
Home Economists: Emma Jane Frost, Teresa Goldfinch

Contents

Foreword

I know someone who uses his barbecue all year round. 'Whenever there's a fine day, I'll fire it up and cook something,' he told me. 'The only thing that changes is how many clothes I'm wearing – that's the indicator of what the season is. I even got it out one Christmas to roast the turkey, when one of our ovens was on the blink and we didn't have room for everything in the other one.'

I'm going to be taking tips from him and using my barbecue whenever possible now, with this book firmly propped open on the side. If you've never cooked on a barbecue before, flick to the first chapter which includes advice on getting it going and keeping the fire under control and, very importantly, health and safety tips to ensure the food is cooked thoroughly. There are recipes for fish and shellfish, chicken, meat and vegetables, salads and bread to serve alongside, refreshing drinks and some quick desserts. And if you're worried about food prep, we've covered that, too.

Now all that's left for you to do is choose which of the 101 recipes you're going to cook first. All of them have been triple-tested in the Good Housekeeping kitchens to make sure they look and taste delicious every time you make them.

Emma Marsden
Cookery Editor
Good Housekeeping

0

The Basics

Choose your fuel

- Lumpwood charcoal or good-quality charcoal briquettes give out a good heat and cook evenly.
- One of the easiest and least messy barbecue fuels are 'ready in the bag' charcoal briquettes, available from petrol stations and supermarkets. They are very simple to use – just place the bag on the barbecue and light with a match.
- Make sure you choose charcoal from sustainable sources, such as brands accredited by the Forest Stewardship Council (FSC).
- Aromatic wood chips and flavourings are best used with a hooded barbecue so the smoke permeates the food during cooking; in an open barbecue the flavour just burns away.
- A gas barbecue can be expensive to buy, but is easy to control.

Cook's Tip

If the weather lets you down, most of the recipes in this book can be cooked under the grill or in a ridged griddle pan. Preheat the grill for about 10 minutes, the griddle pan for 5–10 minutes – and remember that cooking times may be a bit longer than on a barbecue.

Planning your barbecue

What could be better on a hot summer's day than a barbecue? Food always smells particularly appetising when it's cooking in the open air. But before you invite your friends round, take a little time to make a plan, so you can enjoy yourself while you cook.

Get set

Before you start, make sure the barbecue is clean; a wire brush and warm soapy water should do the trick. If the grill looks particularly grimy, soak it in a solution of soda crystals, scrub with a metal scourer, then rinse and dry well. Make sure you have enough fuel.

A layer of sand in the drip tray of a gas barbecue will make cleaning up much easier.

Next, gather together chopping boards, serving dishes and glasses, cook's knives, basting brushes, tongs, a fork, spatula and a turner, oven gloves, kitchen foil, kitchen paper, paper napkins, water spray, a bucket of water or a fire blanket (to douse any flames), corkscrew and bottle opener.

Cook's Tips

A good set of tools will help your barbecue run smoothly, making it easy to grip and turn food on the grill. Look for dishwasher-safe stainless steel utensils: tongs, a fork and a turner.

A hinged, double-sided grill rack will help turn delicate food such as fish, which can easily fall apart. Larger grill racks are perfect for turning lots of food over at once. These are available from kitchen departments, garden centres and large supermarkets.

Health and safety hints

- Choose a position on solid level ground, away from buildings or fences. Avoid windy areas. Don't leave food on the barbecue unattended.
- Keep children and pets away from the barbecue.
- Tie back long hair and don't wear trailing sleeves or scarves; wear an apron to protect your clothes.
- Use extra-long matches when lighting the fire so your fingers don't get burned.
- Use oven gloves and long-handled barbecue tools for turning food.
- Have a bucket of water or a fire blanket to hand to douse the flames if they get out of control, and a spray water bottle to help stop grease flare ups.
- Leave the embers until completely cold before throwing them away; embers that look grey may still be hot. Cover with a lid, if available, and leave overnight.

Food hygiene

- Never barbecue frozen food; thaw it first.
- Raw poultry and meat contain harmful bacteria that can spread easily to anything they touch.
- Always wash your hands, kitchen surfaces, chopping boards, knives and equipment before and after handling poultry or meat.
- Use separate chopping boards for raw and cooked foods to prevent cross-contamination.
- Don't let raw poultry or meat touch other foods.
- Store raw foods in covered containers out of direct sunshine – cool boxes are perfect.
- Keep different raw foods separate and never mix together in the same marinade.
- Cook vegetarian food on a separate barbecue.

Ready to cook

- Long metal skewers are useful when barbecuing. Wooden or bamboo skewers are an attractive alternative, but always remember to soak them in a bowl of cold water for 20–30 minutes before you use them, to prevent them from burning on the barbecue.
- Take ingredients out of the refrigerator about 30 minutes before cooking to ensure the food cooks quickly and evenly. This is especially important for chicken and pork, which should always be cooked through.
- To prevent food from sticking on the barbecue, grease the grill rack with a little sunflower oil after heating for 10 minutes.
- Brush food with oil or baste with any remaining marinade to keep it moist while cooking.
- Cook fish and meat separately – allow the barbecue to burn freely for a few minutes between fish and meat to remove any food traces.
- Ensure food is cooked thoroughly, especially pork and poultry. It might look cooked on the outside, but may still be raw inside. Test by piercing with a thin skewer; if the juices run clear the meat is cooked through; if not, return to the barbecue or grill for a few minutes. Or use a meat thermometer.
- Resist the urge to poke or prod food too much – this will help preserve its flavour and juices.
- Turn only once during cooking.

Light your fire

- Arrange some firelighters in the bottom of the barbecue. Pile the charcoal in a pyramid about 5–7.5cm (2–3in) high over the top. Light the firelighters with a taper or long match and leave them to get the fire started.
- Light a charcoal barbecue 30–40 minutes before you want to use it so that there are no flames.
- When the coals are burning strongly, spread them out in an even layer and leave until they are glowing red at night or lightly covered in whitish ash in daylight.
- It is essential that you use enough fuel to cook all your food and that the temperature is right. Always get the coals to white heat – glowing and covered with white ash, with no black showing and no flames, as these will burn rather than cook the meat.
- To test how hot the barbecue is, hold your hand about 10cm (4in) above the grill rack. If you can keep your hand there for only one to two seconds, the coals are very hot; if you can manage three to four seconds the coals are medium–hot.
- When you are ready to cook, put the barbecue grid in position to heat up. To keep the charcoal at the right temperature, add fresh charcoal gradually around the edge. Do not add charcoal on top of the fire: it may create flames or excessive smoke.

Nibbles and accompaniments

Have some nibbles ready so your guests don't get too hungry while waiting for the food to be cooked. Raw vegetables such as carrots, celery and cucumber, cut into strips, with one or two simple dips or salsas, are ideal.

All you need to go with the barbecued food are a couple of salads and some bread such as pitta or Griddled Garlic Bread (see page 113).

We've included some ideas for barbecued desserts on pages 116–122. **Toasted marshmallows are a simple treat**: thread on to skewers and grill for 10–20 seconds. Alternatively, prepare a big bowl of strawberries, some sliced pineapple or other fresh fruit, or a fresh fruit tart.

Grilled bread

Bread can be toasted on a barbecue or on a griddle, giving attractive brown lines. Either add bread to the barbecue after the food has cooked, or brush the bread lightly with olive oil and cook on a ridged griddle.

Drinks

Set bottles and cans to chill in a clean dustbin or large bucket filled with cold water and ice. This chills drinks more efficiently than ice on its own. See our simple drinks recipes on pages 123–126.

You can buy ice in bulk from off-licences and some supermarkets, but check in advance as you may need to order it – don't imagine you will be the only person throwing a party on a hot summer's day!

Preparing vegetables

Garlic, chillies and tomatoes are key flavouring ingredients of many barbecue dishes; once you've mastered these basic techniques you'll find them quick and easy to prepare.

Tomatoes

Peeling

1 Fill a bowl or pan with boiling water. Using a slotted spoon, add the tomato for 15–30 seconds, then remove to a chopping board.

2 Use a small sharp knife to cut out the core in a single cone-shaped piece. Discard the core.

3 Peel off the skin; it should come away easily depending on ripeness.

Seeding

Removing the seeds from tomatoes is the first step when making some sauces and marinades.

1 Halve the tomato through the core. Use a small sharp knife or a spoon to remove the seeds and juice. Shake off the excess liquid.

2 Chop the tomato as required for your recipe and place in a colander for a minute or two, to drain off any excess liquid.

Chillies

Always wash your hands thoroughly with soap and water immediately after handling chillies.

1 Cut off the cap and slit open lengthways. Using a spoon, scrape out the seeds and the pith. (These are the hottest parts of the chilli.)

2 For diced chilli, cut into thin shreds lengthways, then cut crossways.

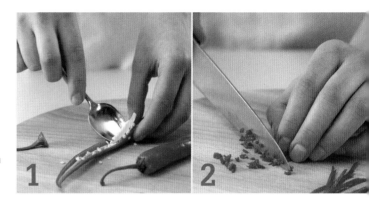

Garlic

1 Put the clove on the chopping board and put the flat side of a large knife on top of it. Press down firmly on the flat of the blade to crush the clove and break the papery skin.

2 Cut off the base of the clove and slip the garlic out of its skin. It should come away easily.

3 **Slicing** Using a rocking motion with the knife tip on the board, slice the garlic as thinly as you need.

4 **Shredding and chopping** Holding the slices together, shred them across the slices. Chop the shreds if you need chopped garlic.

5 **Crushing** After step 2, either use a garlic press or crush with a knife: roughly chop the peeled cloves and put them on the board with a pinch of salt. Press down hard with the edge of a large knife tip (with the blade facing away from you), then drag the blade along the garlic while still pressing hard. Continue to do this, dragging the knife tip over the garlic to make a purée.

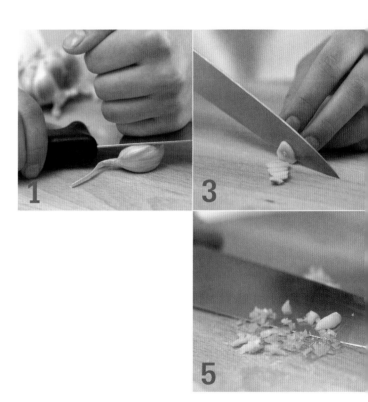

Vegetables to throw on the barbecue

Asparagus	Snap off the woody end of the stem; brush with oil and grill over medium-hot coals for 6–8 minutes until just tender.
Aubergines	Slice, brush with oil and grill over medium-hot coals for 10–15 minutes, turning once or twice, until tender. Alternatively, cut into chunks and thread on to skewers.
Courgettes	Slice, brush with oil and grill over medium-hot coals for 8–10 minutes, turning once, until tender. Alternatively, cut into chunks and thread on to skewers.
Mushrooms	Thread on to skewers, brush with oil and grill over medium-hot coals for 5–6 minutes.
Onions	Thread baby onions on to skewers and grill over medium-hot coals for 10–15 minutes. Cut larger onions into wedges, thread on to skewers, brush with oil and grill over very hot coals for 30–35 minutes.
Peppers	Cut into chunks, brush with oil and grill over medium-hot coals for 8–10 minutes.
Tomatoes	Thread small whole tomatoes or cherry tomatoes on to a skewer and grill over medium-hot coals for about 1 minute or until the skins begin to blister and burst. Larger tomatoes can be halved, sprinkled with finely chopped garlic, salt and pepper and cooked under a hot grill for 6–8 minutes, until tender.

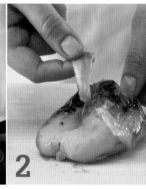

Chargrilling peppers

Charring imparts a smoky flavour and makes peppers easier to peel. Once peeled, they can be cut into strips and drizzled with olive oil, salt and pepper for a simple salad.

1 Hold the pepper, using tongs, over the gas flame on your hob. Alternatively, place on an oiled barbecue grill rack or under a preheated grill. Turn frequently, until the skin blackens all over.

2 Put in a bowl, cover and leave to cool (the steam will help to loosen the skin). Peel.

Slicing aubergines

1 Trim the aubergine to remove the stalk and end. Hold the aubergine upright on a board and cut down.

Grilling and griddling

A few vegetables are perfect for cooking on a griddle or under the grill. Courgettes and aubergines work well in both methods. Peppers (whole or halved) can be grilled and so can fennel, onions and sweet potatoes with careful slicing. Use a medium-high heat.

1 Preheat the griddle over a medium to high heat. Cut the vegetables either lengthways or crossways into 5mm (¼in) slices. Brush with oil.

2 Cook the vegetables without disturbing them until they have deep brown seared lines underneath: about 2–3 minutes.

3 Turn them and griddle until seared underneath; courgettes should be tender but still have a hint of bite; aubergines should be more tender.

Perfect griddled vegetables

- Vegetables have a lovely flavour when cooked on the griddle as well as attractive browned lines if you use a ridged griddle.
- You need to choose vegetables with a fairly even surface that will lie flat on the griddle and won't break up when turned. Top choices include sliced courgettes, aubergines, fennel and onion, whole small onions, large field mushrooms and asparagus.
- Don't slice the vegetables too thickly or they will burn before they get fully cooked – 1cm (½in) should be the maximum thickness.
- Lay the vegetables on a board and brush them with oil to coat them thoroughly.
- Cook on a preheated griddle and turn only once, after they have browned underneath.

Preparing fish and shellfish

Fish and shellfish are perfect grilled or cooked on the barbecue, as the high heat quickly seals the succulent flesh inside a tasty outer layer.

Choosing fish

Whole fish such as sardines, red mullet, mackerel and sea bass are particularly good barbecued.
Steaks of salmon, tuna, swordfish or halibut are perfect for barbecuing – marinate them first for best results.
Thick fillets and steaks of firm white fish such as cod and halibut are suitable for grilling.
Flat fish such as sole and plaice are excellent cooked under the grill, but are too delicate to be cooked directly on the barbecue.
Prawns are ideal either grilled or barbecued. Shelled prawns should be marinated and threaded on to skewers; large prawns can be cooked in their shells – messy to eat but very tasty.

Cleaning round fish

Most fishmongers will clean fish for you, but it is very simple to clean them yourself.

1 Cut off the fins with scissors. Using the blunt edge of a knife, scrape the fish from tail to head and rinse off the loose scales. (The scaled fish should feel smooth.)

2 Insert a sharp knife at the hole towards the rear of the stomach and slit the skin up to the gills. Ease out the entrails. Use scissors to snip out anything that remains. With the knife, cut along the vein under the backbone.

3 Wash the cavity under running water.

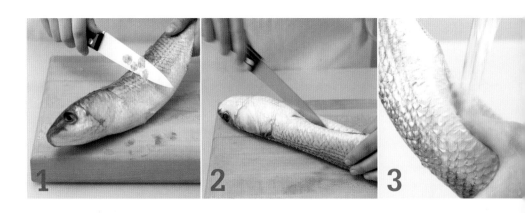

Peeling and butterflying prawns

Raw prawns can be cooked in or out of their shells; some recipes call for them to be 'butterflied'.

1 To shell prawns, pull off the head and put to one side (it can be used later for making stock). Using pointed scissors, cut through the soft shell on the belly side.

2 Prise the shell off, leaving the tail attached. (Put the shell to one side, with the head.)

3 Using a small sharp knife, make a shallow cut along the length of the back of the prawn.

4 Using the point of the knife, carefully remove and discard the black vein (the intestinal tract) that runs along the back of the prawn.

5 To 'butterfly' the prawn, cut halfway through the flesh lengthways from the head end to the base of the tail, and open up the prawn.

Hygiene

Raw poultry and meat contain harmful bacteria that can spread easily to anything they touch.
Always wash your hands, kitchen surfaces, chopping boards, knives and equipment before and after handling poultry or meat.
Don't let raw poultry or meat touch other foods.
Always cover raw poultry and meat, and store in the bottom of the refrigerator, where it can't touch or drip on to other foods.

Preparing poultry

Chicken is a popular and versatile choice for the barbecue; it lends itself to a huge range of flavourings, marinades and sauces and can be cooked in a variety of ways.

Spatchcocking

A technique to flatten smaller poultry and guinea fowl for grilling or cooking on the barbecue.

1 Hold the bird on a board, breast down. Cut through one side of the backbone with poultry shears. Repeat on the other side and remove the backbone.

2 Turn the bird over, then press down until you hear the breastbone crack.

3 Thread skewers through the legs and breasts.

Cooking chicken

Grilling is a perfect way to cook pieces of poultry such as breast fillets or strips or chunks threaded on to skewers.

1   Marinate (see page 24) the poultry pieces for at least 30 minutes, drain and pat dry. Alternatively, brush the poultry with a flavoured oil.

2   Put the pieces on a wire rack over a grill pan or roasting tin, and set the pan under a preheated grill so that it is about 7.5cm (3in) from the heat source. Alternatively, place directly on an oiled barbecue rack.

3   Every few minutes brush a little of the marinade or a teaspoon of oil over the poultry.

4   When cooked on one side, turn with tongs and cook the other side until cooked through. Avoid piercing the flesh when turning – if the juices run out the cooked flesh may be dry.

Grilling times

Turn the chicken two or three times during cooking.

Kebabs	8–12 minutes
Thighs	10–15 minutes
Breast fillet	10–20 minutes
Spatchcocked bird	20–30 minutes

Cook's Tip

Always test that chicken is cooked all the way through, even if it looks cooked on the outside. Test by piercing the thickest part of the meat with a thin skewer; if the juices run clear the meat is cooked through; if not, return to the barbecue or grill for a few minutes.

1

2

Tenderising

Some cuts of steak benefit from tenderising before you grill them. There are two ways to do it: by pounding or scoring.

1 **Pounding** Lay the steaks in a single layer on a large piece of clingfilm or waxed paper. Lay another sheet on top of the slices and pound gently with a rolling pin, small frying pan or the flat side of a meat mallet.

2 **Scoring** is useful for cuts that have long, tough fibres, such as flank. It allows a marinade to penetrate more deeply. Lay the steak on the chopping board and, using a long, very sharp knife, make shallow cuts in one direction across the surface. Make another set of cuts at a 45 degree angle to the first. Now turn the meat over and repeat on the other side.

Preparing meat

Sizzling sausages, succulent lamb chops or juicy steaks are often the highlight of the barbecue. These tips will ensure your meat is cooked the way you like it.

Perfect griddled meat

- Get the griddle smoking hot before putting on the meat.
- You may find that you can cook without oil as long as you let the meat sear thoroughly before turning.
- Put the meat on the griddle and leave for about half the time suggested in the chart (right). When it is cooked it will be easy to turn, so if it seems to be sticking leave for another 30 seconds–1 minute.

Cook's Tip

Boiling sausages before you barbecue them saves cooking time and reduces the risk of burning on the barbecue.

Put the sausages in a pan of boiling water, bring back to the boil and simmer gently for 3 minutes, then drain and leave to cool completely. Barbecue for 7–8 minutes.

Grilling times

These cooking guidelines are useful whether you are cooking meat on the barbecue, a griddle or under a hot grill. These are total cooking times; turn the meat once during cooking. Timings are approximate, for a piece of meat 2.5cm (1in) thick.

Cut	Rare	Medium	Well done
Beef fillet	3–5 minutes	6–7 minutes	8–10 minutes
Other beef steaks	5–6 minutes	8–12 minutes	15–18 minutes
Lamb chops/steaks	8–10 minutes	10–14 minutes	
Lamb cutlets	6–10 minutes	8–12 minutes	
Boned leg of lamb	35–40 minutes	45–50 minutes	
Pork chops/steaks	8–10 minutes	10–14 minutes	
Sausages (see Cook's Tip)		10–15 minutes	

Marinades

One of the best ways to get ahead when barbecuing or grilling food is to marinate it overnight so that the flavour of the marinade has time to permeate the food. If you're in a rush, you should allow at least 30 minutes to 1 hour for the marinade to flavour the food.

Seven super marinades

Quick and Easy

Combine olive oil, lemon or lime juice and chopped garlic, pour over vegetables, fish or shellfish, chicken or meat and marinate in the refrigerator for at least 1 hour.

Lemon and Rosemary

Mix together the coarsely grated zest and juice of 1 lemon with 2 tbsp roughly chopped fresh rosemary and 6 tbsp olive oil. Use for vegetables, fish, chicken or lamb.

Spicy Tomato

Mix together 8 tbsp tomato ketchup with 2 tbsp soy sauce, 2 tbsp chilli sauce and 4 tbsp red wine. Add 2 tsp Jamaican jerk seasoning. Use for chicken, pork or sausages.

Pineapple and Coconut

Blend $1/4$ peeled chopped pineapple with the scooped-out flesh of $1/2$ a lime until smooth. Add 200ml (7fl oz) coconut milk and 1 tsp Tabasco sauce. Use for chicken or pork.

Mustard and Beer

Mix 4 tbsp wholegrain mustard with 150ml ($1/4$ pint) beer. Use for beef steaks or pork.

Hot and Spicy

Combine 1 crushed garlic clove, 2 tbsp ground coriander, 2 tbsp ground cumin, 1 tbsp paprika, 1 seeded and chopped red chilli, the juice of $1/2$ lemon, 2 tbsp soy sauce and 8 thyme sprigs. Use for chicken, pork or lamb.

Tamarind Glaze

Mix 3 tbsp tamarind paste with 2 tbsp clear honey and 1 tbsp dark soy sauce. Use for pork chops or steaks.

Top tips

- Use a large, sealable plastic bag when marinating food: it coats the food more easily, cuts down on washing up, and takes up less space in the refrigerator than a bowl.
- Marinades will not penetrate poultry skin, so remove the skin or cut slashes in it before mixing the poultry with the marinade.
- Use just enough marinade to coat poultry or meat generously: it is wasteful to use too much, as most will be left in the bottom of the container. It cannot be reused once it has been in contact with raw flesh.
- Dry marinated meat to remove liquid from the surface before cooking. Shake off excess marinade and pat dry with kitchen towel.
- Pay attention when using marinades or sweet glazes made with sugar or honey, as they tend to burn if not watched carefully.

Spice rubs

Sometimes referred to as a dry marinade, spice rubs are a great way to add flavour to meat and poultry. They don't penetrate far into the flesh, but give an excellent flavour on and just under the crust. Make them with crushed garlic, dried herbs or spices, and plenty of freshly ground black pepper. Rub into the meat and marinate for at least 30 minutes or up to 8 hours.

Even quicker

Ready made tikka and teriyaki marinades are perfect for most kinds of poultry and meat as well as 'meaty' fish such as tuna.

Flavoured oils – look for lemon, garlic, basil and chilli flavours – can be used as a marinade. Alternatively, just brush the oil over the food before you grill it.

The Ultimate Barbecue Sauce

Quick to make, this sauce goes well with chicken, pork, burgers or sausages.

To make 300ml ($^1/_2$ pint), you will need:
3 tbsp olive oil, 3 garlic cloves, finely chopped, 3 tbsp balsamic vinegar, 4 tbsp dry sherry, 3 tbsp sun-dried tomato paste or tomato purée, 3 tbsp sweet chilli sauce, 300ml ($^1/_2$ pint) passata, 5 tbsp clear honey.

1 In a bowl, mix together the oil, garlic, vinegar, sherry, tomato paste or purée and the chilli sauce. Pour into a pan, then add the passata and honey. Bring to the boil and simmer for 10–15 minutes until thick.

Sauces

Even the simplest grills and barbecued food can be set off with a sauce. Sauces not only add flavour and moisture, they can also bring colour and – if made with vegetables such as tomatoes – nutritional benefits.

Six quick sauces

Mango Mayo

Put the flesh of 1 large mango into a bowl and mash together with 2 tsp freshly chopped coriander, 1 tsp grated fresh root ginger and the juice of 1 lime. Season with salt and pepper. Gradually whisk in 200ml (7fl oz) sunflower oil until thick. Great with barbecued chicken or gammon.

Smoky Pepper Mayo

Whiz 1 peeled chopped grilled red pepper with 1 garlic clove and 250ml (9fl oz) mayonnaise. Stir in 2 tsp chilli oil and 2 tbsp lemon juice. Great with barbecued pork or sausages.

Basil Mayo

Stir 2 tbsp basil pesto into 200ml (7fl oz) mayonnaise. Great with barbecued chicken.

Avocado Salsa

To serve four to six, you will need:
3 large ripe tomatoes, 1 large red pepper, 2 small red chillies, 1 red onion, finely chopped, 4 tbsp freshly chopped coriander, 2 tbsp freshly chopped parsley, 2 ripe avocados, salt and ground black pepper.

1 Quarter, seed and dice the tomatoes. Core, seed and finely chop the pepper. Halve, seed and finely chop the chillies (see page 15) and combine with the tomatoes, peppers, onion and herbs.

2 Halve, stone, peel and dice the avocados. Add to the salsa and season well with salt and pepper. Toss well and serve within about 10 minutes. (Cut avocado flesh will discolour if left for longer than this.)

Avocado Crush

Toss 1 large peeled chopped avocado in 4 tbsp lemon juice. Blend with 100ml (3¹/₂fl oz) olive oil and 2 tbsp water. Great with chicken, fish or any salad.

Mustard and Caper

Mash the yolks of 2 hard-boiled eggs with 2 tsp smooth Dijon mustard. Add 2 tbsp white wine vinegar and gradually whisk in 8 tbsp olive oil. Add 2 tbsp chopped capers, 1 tbsp chopped shallot and a pinch of sugar. Season with salt and pepper. Great with barbecued fish, beef, pork or sausages.

Almond and Herb Pesto

Whiz together 50g (2oz) flat-leafed parsley, 1 thick slice stale bread (crust removed), 2 tbsp lemon juice and 1–2 garlic cloves, then whiz in 50g (2oz) toasted almonds and 200ml (7fl oz) olive oil. Great with barbecued vegetables or chicken, or with pasta.

Flavoured butter

A pat of flavoured butter makes an instant sauce for simply grilled fish, chicken, meat or vegetables.

You will need: 25g (1oz) soft unsalted butter per serving, plus flavouring (see below).

1 Beat the softened butter together with the flavouring. Turn out on to clingfilm, shape into a log, and wrap tightly.

2 Chill in the refrigerator for at least 1 hour. Keep for up to 1 week (or freeze for up to 1 month).

Flavourings
For 125g (4oz) unsalted butter.
Anchovy butter: 6 mashed anchovy fillets.
Herb butter: 2 tbsp finely chopped herbs, a squeeze of lemon juice.
Garlic butter: 1 crushed garlic clove, 2 tsp finely chopped fresh parsley.

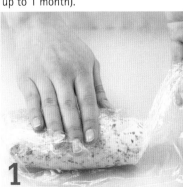

Food storage and hygiene

Storing food properly and preparing food in a hygienic way is important to ensure that food remains as nutritious and flavourful as possible, and to reduce the risk of food poisoning.

Hygiene

When you are preparing food, always follow these important guidelines:

Wash your hands thoroughly before handling food and again between handling different types of food, such as raw and cooked meat and poultry. If you have any cuts or grazes on your hands, be sure to keep them covered with a waterproof plaster.

Wash down worksurfaces regularly with a mild detergent solution or multi-surface cleaner.

Use a dishwasher if available. Otherwise, wear rubber gloves for washing-up, so that the water temperature can be hotter than unprotected hands can bear. Change drying-up cloths and cleaning cloths regularly. Note that leaving dishes to drain is more hygienic than drying them with a teatowel.

Keep raw and cooked foods separate, especially meat, fish and poultry. Wash kitchen utensils in between preparing raw and cooked foods. Never put cooked or ready-to-eat foods directly on to a surface which has just had raw fish, meat or poultry on it.

Keep pets out of the kitchen if possible; or make sure they stay away from worksurfaces. Never allow animals on to worksurfaces.

Shopping

Always choose fresh ingredients in prime condition from stores and markets that have a regular turnover of stock to ensure you buy the freshest produce possible.

Make sure items are within their 'best before' or 'use by' date. (Foods with a longer shelf life have a 'best before' date; more perishable items have a 'use by' date.)

Pack frozen and chilled items in an insulated cool bag at the check-out and put them into the freezer or refrigerator as soon as you get home.

During warm weather in particular, buy perishable foods just before you return home. When packing items at the check-out, sort them according to where you will store them when you get home – the refrigerator, freezer, storecupboard, vegetable, rack, fruit bowl, etc. This will make unpacking easier – and quicker.

The storecupboard

Although storecupboard ingredients will generally last a long time, correct storage is important:

Always check packaging for storage advice – even with familiar foods, because storage requirements may change if additives, sugar or salt have been reduced. Check storecupboard foods for their 'best before' or 'use by' date and do not use them if the date has passed.

Keep all food cupboards scrupulously clean and make sure food containers and packets are properly sealed.

Once opened, treat canned foods as though fresh. Always transfer the contents to a clean container, cover and keep in the refrigerator. Similarly, jars, sauce bottles and cartons should be kept chilled after opening. (Check the label for safe storage times after opening.)

Transfer dry goods such as sugar, rice and pasta to moisture-proof containers. When supplies are used up, wash the container well and thoroughly dry before refilling with new supplies.

Store oils in a dark cupboard away from any heat source as heat and light can make them turn rancid and affect their colour. For the same reason, buy olive oil in dark green bottles.

Store vinegars in a cool place; they can turn bad in a warm environment.

Store dried herbs, spices and flavourings in a cool, dark cupboard or in dark jars. Buy in small quantities as their flavour will not last indefinitely.

Store flours and sugars in airtight containers.

Refrigerator storage

Fresh food needs to be kept in the cool temperature of the refrigerator to keep it in good condition and discourage the growth of harmful bacteria. Store day-to-day perishable items, such as opened jams and jellies, mayonnaise and bottled sauces, in the refrigerator along with eggs and dairy products, fruit juices, bacon, fresh and cooked meat (on separate shelves), and salads and vegetables (except potatoes, which don't suit being stored in the cold). A refrigerator should be kept at an operating temperature of 4–5°C. It is worth investing in a refrigerator thermometer to ensure the correct temperature is maintained.

To ensure your refrigerator is functioning effectively for safe food storage, follow these guidelines:

To avoid bacterial cross-contamination, store cooked and raw foods on separate shelves, putting cooked foods on the top shelf. Ensure that all items are well wrapped.

Never put hot food into the refrigerator, as this will cause the internal temperature of the refrigerator to rise.

Avoid overfilling the refrigerator, as this restricts the circulation of air and prevents the appliance from working properly.

It can take some time for the refrigerator to return to the correct operating temperature once the door has been opened, so don't leave it open any longer than is necessary.

Clean the refrigerator regularly, using a specially formulated germicidal refrigerator cleaner. Alternatively, use a weak solution of bicarbonate of soda: 1 tbsp to 1 litre (1³/₄ pints) water.

If your refrigerator doesn't have an automatic defrost facility, defrost regularly.

Maximum refrigerator storage times

For pre-packed foods, always adhere to the 'use-by' date on the packet. For other foods the following storage times should apply, providing the food is in prime condition when it goes into the refrigerator and that your refrigerator is in good working order:

Vegetables and Fruit

Green vegetables	3–4 days
Salad leaves	2–3 days
Hard and stone fruit	3–7 days
Soft fruit	1–2 days

Dairy Food

Cheese, hard	1 week
Cheese, soft	2–3 days
Eggs	1 week
Milk	4–5 days

Fish

Fish	1 day
Shellfish	1 day

Raw Meat

Bacon	7 days
Game	2 days
Joints	3 days
Minced meat	1 day
Offal	1 day
Poultry	2 days
Raw sliced meat	2 days
Sausages	3 days

Cooked Meat

Joints	3 days
Casseroles/stews	2 days
Pies	2 days
Sliced meat	2 days
Ham	2 days
Ham, vacuum-packed (or according to the instructions on the packet)	1–2 weeks

1

Fish and Shellfish

Cook's Tip

Chillies vary enormously in strength, from quite mild to blisteringly hot, depending on the type of chilli and its ripeness. Taste a small piece first to check it's not too hot for you.

Be extremely careful when handling chillies not to touch or rub your eyes with your fingers, as they will sting. Wash knives immediately after handling chillies for the same reason. As a precaution, use rubber gloves when preparing them if you like.

Saffron and Lime Prawns

finely grated zest and juice of 1 lime

a large pinch of saffron

1 garlic clove, crushed

2 small red chillies, seeded and very finely chopped (see Cook's Tip)

75ml (3fl oz) extra virgin olive oil

32 raw tiger prawns, deveined and peeled

salad and pitta bread or Griddled Garlic Bread (see page 113) to serve

1 Put the lime zest and juice into a small pan and heat gently. Add the saffron and leave to soak for 5 minutes. Stir in the garlic and chillies and add the olive oil. Pour into a screwtopped jar, secure the lid tightly and shake well.

2 Put the prawns in a shallow dish, add the marinade, cover and leave for at least 1 hour.

3 Preheat the barbecue or grill. Soak eight bamboo skewers in water for 20 minutes.

4 Thread four prawns on each skewer. Lay the skewers on the barbecue or grill and cook for about 2 minutes on each side until they've just turned pink. Serve immediately, with salad and warm pitta bread or griddled garlic bread.

Serves 8	EASY		NUTRITIONAL INFORMATION	
	Preparation Time 10 minutes, plus minimum 1 hour marinating	**Cooking Time** 4 minutes	**Per Serving** 37 calories, 2g fat (of which trace saturates), 0g carbohydrate, 0.2g salt	Gluten free • Dairy free

6 tbsp groundnut oil

200ml (7fl oz) coconut milk

2 tsp mild chilli powder

3 garlic cloves, finely chopped

30 raw prawns, deveined and peeled, with tail left on

salt and ground black pepper

For the chilli sauce

1 tbsp olive oil

2 large garlic cloves, finely chopped

2 tsp tomato purée

550g (1¼lb) tomatoes, cut into chunks

4 large red chillies, seeded and finely chopped (see page 32)

200g (7oz) dark muscovado sugar

100ml (3½fl oz) white wine vinegar

Chilli Prawns with Sweet Chilli Sauce

1 In a large bowl, mix together the groundnut oil, coconut milk, chilli powder, garlic and ½ tsp each of salt and pepper. Add the prawns, tossing to coat evenly. Cover and marinate for at least 2 hours at room temperature or overnight in the refrigerator.

2 Meanwhile, make the chilli sauce. Heat the olive oil in a pan, add the garlic and tomato purée and cook for 30 seconds. Add the tomatoes, chillies, sugar and vinegar. Bring to the boil and bubble for 30–35 minutes until reduced and pulpy. Pour the tomato mixture into a sieve and, using the back of a ladle, push through as much of the pulp as possible. Return to the pan and simmer for 5 minutes. Add salt to taste. Set aside.

3 Preheat the barbecue or grill. Soak six wooden skewers in water for 20 minutes. Thread five prawns on each skewer and barbecue or grill for 3–4 minutes on each side, basting with the marinade. Serve with the chilli sauce for dipping.

EASY		NUTRITIONAL INFORMATION		Serves
Preparation Time 40 minutes, plus soaking and 2 hours marinating	**Cooking Time** 50 minutes	**Per Serving** 211 calories, 4g fat (of which 1g saturates), 38g carbohydrate, 0.2g salt	Gluten free • Dairy free	**6**

Prawn and Fish Kebabs

4 long, strong stalks of fresh rosemary (see Cook's Tips)

2 garlic cloves, crushed

6 tbsp olive oil

350g (12oz) firm white fish, such as cod, cut into bite-size pieces

175g (6oz) large raw prawns, peeled

grated zest and juice of 1 lemon

8 thin rashers smoked streaky bacon or pancetta

about 350g (12oz) tzatziki (see Cook's Tips)

1 lemon or lime, cut into wedges, to serve

couscous and freshly chopped flat-leafed parsley to serve

1 Preheat the barbecue or grill. Strip almost all the leaves from the rosemary, apart from the top 5cm (2in). Roughly chop the stripped leaves and mix with the garlic and oil. Stir in the fish, prawns, lemon zest and juice.

2 Cut the bare tip of each rosemary stalk to a sharp point, then use to skewer the fish and prawns. Loosely wrap two bacon or pancetta rashers around each kebab, weaving them around the fish and prawns.

3 Cook the kebabs for about 3 minutes on each side if using pancetta, or 5 minutes if using bacon, until the fish is opaque and the bacon is cooked. Season and serve with tzatziki and lemon or lime wedges, plus couscous with some freshly chopped flat-leafed parsley stirred through.

Cook's Tips

If you can't find strong rosemary stalks, use wooden skewers. Soak in cold water for 20 minutes before use to prevent them from burning.

Add chopped cucumber and fresh mint to natural yogurt, or use plain yogurt, if you can't find ready-made tzatziki.

EASY		NUTRITIONAL INFORMATION		Serves
Preparation Time 25 minutes	**Cooking Time** 10 minutes	**Per Serving** 341 calories, 21g fat (of which 8g saturates), 2g carbohydrate, 2.9g salt	Gluten free	**4**

Get Ahead

Complete the recipe to the end of step 2 and chill for
24 hours.
To use Complete the recipe.

Steam-grilled Oriental Salmon

sesame oil to grease

4 salmon fillets, about 150g (5oz) each and
2.5cm (1in) thick

4 tbsp soy sauce

200g (7oz) pak choi or spinach

2.5cm (1in) piece fresh root ginger, coarsely grated

4 spring onions, sliced

fresh coriander sprigs to garnish

Thai rice to serve

1   Preheat the barbecue or grill. Lightly grease four
large sheets of foil, each about 35.5cm (14in) square,
with sesame oil. Put a salmon fillet in the centre of
each piece of foil and drizzle with 1 tbsp soy sauce.

2   Divide the pak choi or spinach leaves, ginger and
spring onions among the salmon fillets, then fold up
the foil loosely but neatly to form parcels. Seal the
edges well so the parcels can be turned over during
cooking; make sure the foil parcels are large enough
to allow for the expansion of air that takes place as
the salmon begins to cook.

3   Place the parcels on the barbecue or under a hot grill
and cook for 4–5 minutes on each side. Serve the
sealed parcels to your guests at the table – warn
them to watch out as they open the parcels, though,
as the steam builds up inside. Garnish with coriander
sprigs and serve with fragrant Thai rice.

Serves 4	EASY		NUTRITIONAL INFORMATION	
	Preparation Time 15 minutes	**Cooking Time** 10 minutes	**Per Serving** 291 calories, 17g fat (of which 3g saturates), 2g carbohydrate, 3g salt	Gluten free • Dairy free

Lime and Chilli Swordfish

1 tsp dried chilli flakes

4 tbsp olive oil

grated zest and juice of 1 lime, plus 1 whole lime, sliced, to serve

1 garlic clove, crushed

4 x 175g (6oz) swordfish steaks

salt and ground black pepper

mixed salad to serve

1 Put the chilli flakes in a large shallow bowl. Add the olive oil, lime zest, juice and garlic and mix everything together. Add the swordfish steaks to the marinade and toss several times to coat completely. Leave to marinate for 30 minutes.

2 Preheat the barbecue or preheat a griddle pan until hot.

3 Lift the swordfish out of the marinade, season well with salt and pepper, then cook the steaks for 2 minutes on each side. Top with slices of lime and continue to cook for 1 minute or until the fish is opaque right through. Serve immediately, with a mixed salad.

EASY		NUTRITIONAL INFORMATION		Serves
Preparation Time 10 minutes, plus 30 minutes marinating	**Cooking Time** 10 minutes	**Per Serving** 216 calories, 10g fat (of which 2g saturates), 0g carbohydrate, 0.6g salt	Gluten free • Dairy free	**4**

Lemon Tuna

3 large lemons
2 garlic cloves, crushed
100ml (3½fl oz) extra virgin olive oil
900g (2lb) fresh tuna in one piece
3 tbsp freshly chopped flat-leafed parsley
ground black pepper
flatbread to serve

1 Finely grate the zest from one lemon and squeeze the juice from the grated lemon and one other lemon. Mix the zest and juice with the garlic and olive oil and season well with pepper.

2 Cut the tuna in half lengthways, then cut into strips about 2cm (¾ in) thick. Lay the strips in a shallow dish, pour the marinade over, then turn the fish to coat. Cover and leave for at least 30 minutes.

3 Preheat the barbecue or grill. Soak eight bamboo skewers in water for 20 minutes.

4 Fold the strips of tuna and thread on to the skewers. Cut the remaining lemon into eight wedges and push one on to each skewer. Drizzle with any remaining marinade and sprinkle over the chopped parsley.

5 Lay the skewers on the barbecue or grill and cook for 2–3 minutes on each side. Serve immediately with warmed flatbread.

Serves 8	EASY		NUTRITIONAL INFORMATION	
	Preparation Time 15–20 minutes, plus 30 minutes marinating	**Cooking Time** 4–6 minutes	**Per Serving** 180 calories, 8g fat (of which 2g saturates), trace carbohydrate, 0.1g salt	Gluten free • Dairy free

Get Ahead

Complete the recipe to the end of step 1, cover and chill for up to 3 hours.
To use Stir-fry the vegetables for 2–3 minutes or until hot. Complete the recipe.

Sardines with Mediterranean Vegetables

3 tbsp olive oil

2 red onions, about 300g (11oz), peeled, halved and cut into petals

2 garlic cloves, crushed

2 red peppers, about 375g (12oz), halved, seeded and cut into chunks

225g (8oz) courgettes, cut into small chunks

900g (2lb) sardines (about 16), cleaned

olive oil and lemon juice to drizzle

salt and ground black pepper

small fresh basil sprigs to garnish

1 Heat the olive oil in a large griddle pan or preheat the grill. Add the onion and fry for 2–3 minutes until almost soft. Add the garlic and peppers and stir-fry for 5 minutes, then add the courgettes and stir-fry for 4–5 minutes until almost soft. Remove from the griddle and keep warm.

2 Season the sardines and cook on the griddle or under a hot grill for 3–4 minutes on each side until cooked in the centre.

3 Drizzle the sardines with a little olive oil and lemon juice. Garnish with basil and serve with the vegetables.

Serves	EASY		NUTRITIONAL INFORMATION	
4	**Preparation Time** 15 minutes	**Cooking Time** 20 minutes	**Per Serving** 409 calories, 23g fat (of which 5g saturates), 13g carbohydrate, 0.5g salt	Gluten free • Dairy free

Cook's Tip

Barbecued Red Peppers: halve 3 red peppers, remove the seeds, then cut into thick strips. Brush with 1 tbsp olive oil and season with salt and pepper. Cook on the barbecue or on a preheated griddle for 15–20 minutes until the peppers are tender.

Garlic and Thyme Fish Steaks

2 garlic cloves, crushed

2 tbsp chopped thyme leaves

4 tbsp olive oil

2 lemons

4 x 200g (7oz) firm fish steaks, such as tuna, swordfish or shark

salt and ground black pepper

Barbecued Red Peppers (see Cook's Tip) and salad leaves to serve

1 Put the garlic, thyme, olive oil and the juice of one lemon in a large shallow container and mix together well.

2 Add the fish steaks and season with salt and pepper, then cover and chill for 20 minutes. Cut the other lemon into four slices and put to one side.

3 Preheat the barbecue or a griddle pan.

4 Cook the fish on the barbecue or griddle, for 4–5 minutes on one side and brush over a little of the marinade. Turn over, put a slice of reserved lemon on top of each steak and continue to cook for 3–4 minutes or until cooked through. Serve with Barbecued Red Peppers and salad leaves.

EASY		NUTRITIONAL INFORMATION		Serves
Preparation Time 10 minutes, plus 20 minutes marinating	**Cooking Time** 5–10 minutes	**Per Serving** 299 calories, 12g fat (of which 3g saturates), trace carbohydrate, 0.2g salt	Gluten free • Dairy free	**4**

Try Something Different

Instead of tarragon, use dill. Replace salmon with halibut fillets.

2–4 tsp oil
4 wild salmon fillets, about 175g (6oz) each
lemon halves to serve

For the tarragon mayonnaise
1 large egg yolk
½ tsp English mustard powder
75ml (3fl oz) each sunflower and olive oil
2 tbsp freshly chopped tarragon, plus a few leaves to garnish
squeeze of lemon juice
salt and ground black pepper
lemon halves to serve

Wild Salmon with Tarragon Mayonnaise

1 To make the mayonnaise, put the egg yolk in a bowl and mix with a balloon whisk. Add the mustard powder and mix again. Very slowly, add tiny amounts of the sunflower and olive oils to the egg, briefly whisking between each addition, until all the oil is used and the mixture is thick. Stir in the tarragon and a generous squeeze of lemon juice and season well with salt and pepper.

2 Heat the oil in a griddle pan until very hot. Season the salmon with salt and pepper, then cook in the pan, skin side down, for about 5 minutes until the lower half of each piece turns pale pink. Turn and continue to cook over a medium heat for 3–4 minutes until just cooked – the salmon should still be slightly pink in the middle. Sprinkle with pepper and a few tarragon leaves and serve with the mayonnaise and lemon halves to squeeze over.

Serves 4	EASY		NUTRITIONAL INFORMATION	
	Preparation Time 15 minutes	Cooking Time 9 minutes	Per Serving 599 calories, 50g fat (of which 8g saturates), 1g carbohydrate, 0.2g salt	Gluten free • Dairy free

Swordfish with Green Beans and Pistachios

juice of ½ lemon

125ml (4fl oz) extra virgin olive oil, plus extra to drizzle

4 x 175g (6oz) swordfish steaks

3 large ripe tomatoes, cut into wedges

1–2 tbsp freshly chopped oregano

1 garlic clove, crushed

250g (9oz) fine green beans

100g (3½oz) shelled pistachio nuts

salt and ground black pepper

1 Put the lemon juice in a shallow dish, then add 2 tbsp olive oil and mix together well. Add the swordfish and turn to coat, then cover and put in the refrigerator to marinate for at least 30 minutes.

2 Put the tomatoes in a large bowl, add the oregano, the remaining oil and the garlic and season with salt and pepper.

3 Bring a large pan of salted water to the boil and cook the beans for 3–5 minutes until tender. Drain well and add to the bowl with the tomatoes. Add the pistachio nuts and toss together.

4 Preheat a griddle pan. Lift the swordfish out of the marinade, season with salt and pepper and cook over a medium heat for 3–4 minutes on each side.

5 Divide the swordfish among four warmed plates, spoon the bean mixture over and drizzle with a little olive oil.

EASY		NUTRITIONAL INFORMATION		Serves
Preparation Time 15 minutes, plus 30 minutes marinating	**Cooking Time** 12 minutes	**Per Serving** 517 calories, 38g fat (of which 6g saturates), 6g carbohydrate, 0.9g salt	Gluten free • Dairy free	**4**

Cod with Sweet Chilli Glaze

1 red chilli, seeded and finely chopped (see page 32)

2 tsp dark soy sauce

grated zest and juice of 1 lime

1/4 tsp ground allspice or 6 allspice berries, crushed

50g (2oz) light muscovado sugar

4 thick cod fillets, with skin, about 175g (6oz) each

finely sliced red chilli, finely sliced lime zest and lime wedges to garnish

For the saffron mash

900g (2lb) potatoes, peeled and chopped

a pinch of saffron

50g (2oz) butter

salt and ground black pepper

1 To make the saffron mash, cook the potatoes in boiling salted water until tender. Meanwhile, soak the saffron in 2 tbsp boiling water. Drain the potatoes and mash with the butter, then beat in the saffron liquid. Season with salt and pepper.

2 Meanwhile, preheat the grill or griddle pan until hot. Stir the chopped chilli, soy sauce, lime zest and juice, allspice and sugar together.

3 Grill the cod for about 1 minute on the flesh side. Turn skin side up and grill for 1 minute. Spoon the chilli glaze over and grill for a further 2–3 minutes until the skin is crisp and golden. Garnish with finely sliced chilli and lime zest and the lime wedges. Serve with saffron mash.

Serves 4	EASY		NUTRITIONAL INFORMATION	
	Preparation Time 10 minutes	**Cooking Time** 20 minutes	**Per Serving** 193 calories, 1g fat (of which trace saturates), 13g carbohydrate, 0.7g salt	Gluten free

2

Chicken

Try Something Different

Pork and Apricot Burgers: replace the chicken with minced pork, use chopped sage instead of tarragon and add 100g (3½oz) chopped ready-to-eat dried apricots to the mixture before shaping.

Chicken Tarragon Burgers

225g (8oz) minced chicken

2 shallots, finely chopped

1 tbsp freshly chopped tarragon

25g (1oz) fresh breadcrumbs

1 large egg yolk

oil to grease

salt and ground black pepper

burger buns, mayonnaise or Greek yogurt, salad leaves and tomato salad to serve

1 Put the chicken in a bowl with the shallots, tarragon, breadcrumbs and egg yolk. Mix well, then beat in about 75ml (3fl oz) cold water and season with salt and pepper.

2 Lightly oil a foil-lined baking sheet. Divide the chicken mixture into four portions and place on the foil. Using the back of a wet spoon, flatten each portion to a thickness of 2.5cm (1in). Cover and chill for 30 minutes.

3 Preheat the barbecue or grill. Cook the burgers for 5–6 minutes on each side or until cooked through, then serve in a toasted burger bun with a dollop of mayonnaise or Greek yogurt, a few salad leaves and tomato salad.

Serves 2	EASY		NUTRITIONAL INFORMATION	
	Preparation Time 30 minutes, plus 30 minutes chilling	**Cooking Time** 12 minutes	**Per Serving** 205 calories, 4g fat (of which 1g saturates), 12g carbohydrate, 0.4g salt	Dairy free

Chicken Kebabs with Tabbouleh

1 tbsp balsamic vinegar

6 tbsp olive oil

grated zest of 1 lime and juice of 2 limes

2 garlic cloves, crushed

4 large skinless chicken breasts, approximately 700g (1½lb), cut into 2.5cm (1in) cubes

75g (3oz) bulgur wheat

½ cucumber, halved lengthways, seeded and diced

4 plum tomatoes, seeded and diced

1 small red onion, finely chopped

4 tbsp freshly chopped mint

4 tbsp freshly chopped flat-leafed parsley

ground black pepper

lime wedges and mint sprigs to garnish

1 In a large bowl, whisk together the balsamic vinegar, 3 tbsp olive oil, the zest and juice of 1 lime, and 1 garlic clove. Add the chicken, mix well, then cover and chill for at least 2 hours, preferably overnight.

2 To make the tabbouleh, put the bulgur wheat in a bowl, cover with double its volume of boiling water and leave to soak for 15 minutes. Drain the bulgur wheat, squeeze out the liquid and return to the bowl. Stir in the cucumber, tomatoes, onion and herbs. Season with pepper. In a small bowl, whisk together the remaining olive oil, lime juice and garlic. Add to the bulgur wheat and mix gently but thoroughly until the bulgur is well coated. Cover and chill.

3 Preheat the barbecue, grill or griddle. Soak eight wooden skewers in water for 20 minutes. Remove the chicken from the marinade, thread on to the skewers and cook for 10–12 minutes, turning every now and then, or until cooked through. Serve with the tabbouleh. Garnish with lime wedges and mint sprigs.

EASY		NUTRITIONAL INFORMATION		Serves
Preparation Time 35 minutes, plus minimum 2 hours marinating	**Cooking Time** 5 minutes, plus soaking	**Per Serving** 330 calories, 8g fat (of which 1g saturates), 19g carbohydrate, 0.3g salt	Dairy free	**4**

Chicken Satay Skewers

1 tbsp each coriander and cumin seeds

2 tsp ground turmeric

4 garlic cloves, roughly chopped

grated zest and juice of 1 lemon

2 bird's eye chillies, finely chopped (see page 32)

3 tbsp vegetable oil

4 boneless skinless chicken breasts, around 550g (1¼lb) cut into finger-length strips

salt and ground black pepper

½ cucumber, cut into sticks, to serve

For the satay sauce

200g (7oz) salted peanuts

1 tbsp molasses sugar

½ lemongrass stalk, chopped

2 tbsp dark soy sauce

juice of ½ lime

200ml (7fl oz) coconut cream

1 Put the coriander and cumin seeds and the turmeric in a dry frying pan and heat for 30 seconds. Tip into a blender and add the garlic, lemon zest and juice, chillies, 1 tbsp oil and 1 tsp salt. Whiz for 1–2 minutes.

2 Put the paste in a large shallow dish, add the chicken and toss everything together. Cover and chill for at least 20 minutes or up to 12 hours.

3 To make the satay sauce, put the peanuts, sugar, lemongrass, soy sauce, lime juice and coconut cream in a processor and add 2 tbsp water. Whiz to make a thick chunky sauce, then spoon into a dish. Cover and chill.

4 Preheat the barbecue or grill until hot. Soak 24 bamboo skewers in water for 20 minutes. Thread the chicken on to the skewers, drizzle with the remaining oil and grill for 4–5 minutes on each side or until the juices run clear. Serve with the satay sauce and the cucumber.

Try Something Different

Replace the chicken with strips of pork tenderloin or beef rump.

Serves 4	EASY		NUTRITIONAL INFORMATION	
	Preparation Time 30 minutes, pus 20 minutes chilling	**Cooking Time** 40 minutes	**Per Serving** 687 calories, 51g fat (of which 21g saturates), 11g carbohydrate, 2.1g salt	Gluten free • Dairy free

Menu

▼ Moroccan Spiced Chicken Kebabs
▶ Charred Courgettes (see page 95)
▶ Roasted Rosemary Potatoes (see page 94)
▶ Barbecued Figs with Marsala (see page 116)

Moroccan Spiced Chicken Kebabs

2 tbsp olive oil
15g (½oz) flat-leafed parsley
1 garlic clove
½ tsp paprika
1 tsp ground cumin
grated zest and juice of 1 lemon
4 skinless chicken breasts, cut into bite-size chunks

1 Put the olive oil in a blender and add the parsley, garlic, paprika, cumin, lemon zest and juice. Whiz to make a paste.

2 Put the chicken in a shallow dish and add the spice paste, then rub in and leave to marinate for at least 20 minutes.

3 Preheat the barbecue or grill. Soak four wooden skewers in water for 20 minutes.

4 Thread the marinated chicken on to the skewers and grill for 10–12 minutes, turning every now and then, until cooked through.

Serves 4	EASY		NUTRITIONAL INFORMATION	
	Preparation Time 10 minutes, plus minimum 20 minutes marinating	**Cooking Time** 10–12 minutes	**Per Serving** 189 calories, 5g fat (of which 1g saturates), 1g carbohydrate, 0.2g salt	Gluten free • Dairy free

Garlic and Thyme Chicken

2 garlic cloves, crushed

2 tbsp freshly chopped thyme leaves

2 tbsp olive oil

4 chicken thighs

salt and ground black pepper

1 Preheat the barbecue or grill. Mix together the garlic, thyme and olive oil in a large bowl. Season with salt and pepper.

2 Using a sharp knife, make two or three slits in each chicken thigh. Put the chicken into the bowl and toss to coat thoroughly. Grill for 5–7 minutes on each side until golden and cooked through.

EASY		NUTRITIONAL INFORMATION		Serves
Preparation Time 10 minutes	**Cooking Time** 10–15 minutes	**Per Serving** 135 calories, 6g fat (of which 1g saturates), trace carbohydrate, 0.2g salt	Gluten free • Dairy free	**4**

4 tbsp hot mango chutney (or ordinary mango chutney, plus ½ tsp Tabasco)

grated zest and juice of 1 lime

4 tbsp natural yogurt

2 tbsp freshly chopped coriander

1 small green chilli (optional), seeded and finely chopped (see page 32)

4 chicken breasts with skin on

1 large ripe mango, peeled and stoned

oil to brush

salt and ground black pepper

fresh coriander sprigs and lime wedges to garnish

Fiery Mango Chicken

1   Mix together the chutney, lime zest and juice, yogurt, chopped coriander and, if you like it spicy, the finely chopped chilli.

2   Put the chicken breasts skin side down on the worksurface, cover with clingfilm and lightly beat with a rolling pin. Slice each into three pieces and put into the yogurt mixture; stir to coat. Cover and chill for at least 30 minutes or overnight.

3   Preheat the barbecue or grill. Slice the mango into four thick pieces. Brush lightly with oil and season well with salt and pepper. Barbecue or grill for about 2 minutes on each side; the fruit should be lightly charred but still firm. Put to one side.

4   Barbecue or grill the chicken for 3–5 minutes on each side until golden. Serve with the grilled mango, garnished with coriander and lime wedges.

Serves 4	EASY		NUTRITIONAL INFORMATION	
	Preparation Time 15 minutes, plus minimum 30 minutes marinating	**Cooking Time** 10 minutes	**Per Serving** 220 calories, 8g fat (of which 2g saturates), 7g carbohydrate, 0.3g salt	Gluten free

Try Something Different

Hoisin, Sesame and Orange Marinade: mix together
6 tbsp hoisin sauce, 1 tbsp sesame seeds and the juice of
½ orange. Add the chicken wings and toss to coat.
Middle Eastern Marinade: mix together 3 tbsp harissa
paste, 1 tbsp tomato purée and 3 tbsp olive oil. Stir in a
small handful each of freshly chopped mint and parsley,
add the chicken wings and toss to coat.

Sticky Chicken Wings

4 tbsp clear honey

4 tbsp wholegrain mustard

12 large chicken wings

salt and ground black pepper

grilled corn on the cob and green salad to serve

1 Put the honey and mustard in a large glass dish and
mix together. Add the chicken wings and toss to coat.
Season well with salt and pepper. Cook immediately
or, if you've time, cover, chill and leave to marinate
for about 2 hours.

2 Preheat the barbecue or preheat a grill. Lift the wings
from the marinade and cook for 8–10 minutes on
each side until cooked through. Alternatively, roast in
a preheated oven 200°C (180°C fan oven) mark 6 for
40–45 minutes. Serve hot, with grilled corn and a
green salad.

EASY		NUTRITIONAL INFORMATION		Serves
Preparation Time 10 minutes, plus 2 hours marinating (optional)	**Cooking Time** 20–45 minutes	**Per Serving** 257 calories, 14g fat (of which 4g saturates), 13g carbohydrate, 0.5g salt	Gluten free • Dairy free	**4**

Grilled Spicy Chicken

4 skinless chicken breast fillets

1 tbsp coriander seeds, crushed

1 tsp ground cumin

2 tsp mild curry paste

1 garlic clove, crushed

450g (1lb) yogurt

3 tbsp freshly chopped coriander

salt and ground black pepper

mixed salad, rice and coriander sprigs to serve

1 Prick the chicken breasts all over with a fork, cover with clingfilm and lightly beat with a rolling pin to flatten them slightly.

2 Mix the coriander seeds with the cumin, curry paste, garlic and yogurt in a large shallow dish. Season with salt and pepper, and stir in the chopped coriander.

3 Add the chicken and turn to coat with the spiced yogurt. Cover and leave to marinate in the refrigerator for at least 30 minutes or overnight.

4 Preheat the barbecue or griddle. Lift the chicken out of the marinade and cook over a medium-high heat, turning occasionally, for about 20 minutes or until cooked through. Serve immediately, with rice and a mixed salad, garnished with coriander sprigs.

Serves 4	EASY		NUTRITIONAL INFORMATION	
	Preparation Time 10 minutes, plus 30 minutes marinating	**Cooking Time** about 20 minutes	**Per Serving** 157 calories, 2g fat (of which 1g saturates), 3g carbohydrate, 0.2g salt	Gluten free

Try Something Different

Replace the chicken with 4 duck breasts with skin; score the skin in a criss-cross pattern and grill for 5–8 minutes on each side.

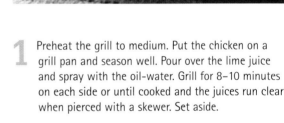

Chicken with Mango and Fennel Salsa

4 skinless chicken breasts

juice of ½ lime

oil-water spray

salt and ground black pepper

rocket to serve

For the salsa

1 mango, peeled, stoned and diced

1 small fennel bulb, trimmed and diced

1 fresh chilli, seeded and finely diced (see page 32)

1 tbsp balsamic vinegar

juice of ½ lime

2 tbsp freshly chopped flat-leafed parsley

2 tbsp freshly chopped mint

1 Preheat the grill to medium. Put the chicken on a grill pan and season well. Pour over the lime juice and spray with the oil-water. Grill for 8–10 minutes on each side or until cooked and the juices run clear when pierced with a skewer. Set aside.

2 Combine all the salsa ingredients in a bowl and season generously with salt and pepper. Spoon on top of the chicken and serve with rocket.

EASY		NUTRITIONAL INFORMATION		Serves
Preparation Time 12 minutes	**Cooking Time** 20 minutes	**Per Serving** 161 calories, 2g fat (of which trace saturates), 6g carbohydrate, 0.2g salt	Gluten free • Dairy free	**4**

Pancetta and Orange-wrapped Chicken

2 garlic cloves

1 tsp sea salt

1 tsp freshly ground black pepper

2 tsp ground coriander

½ tsp ground cumin

finely grated zest of 2 oranges plus juice of ½ orange

12 boneless skinless chicken thighs

12 thin slices pancetta

12 fresh bay leaves

olive oil

1 Preheat the barbecue. Put the garlic, sea salt, pepper and spices in a small bowl and pound to a paste with the end of a rolling pin or use a pestle and mortar. Add the orange zest and juice and mix thoroughly.

2 Rub the paste over the chicken thighs. Carefully stretch the pancetta with the back of a knife. Put a bay leaf in the middle of each slice and put a thigh on top, smooth side down, then fold the ends of the pancetta over so they overlap in the middle. Make sure the bay leaf is well tucked in or it will burn during cooking.

3 Push a cocktail stick through each parcel to secure. Brush generously with olive oil. Barbecue for 20–25 minutes, turning every 5 minutes until golden and cooked through. Serve drizzled with a little extra olive oil and Barbecued Red Peppers (see Cook's Tip page 41).

Menu

▲ Pancetta and Orange-wrapped Chicken
▶ Barbecued Red Peppers (see page 41)
▶ Summer Vegetable Salad (see page 102)
▶ Sweet Kebabs (see page 120)

EASY		NUTRITIONAL INFORMATION		Serves
Preparation Time 30 minutes	**Cooking Time** 20–25 minutes	**Per Serving** 374 calories, 21g fat (of which 7g saturates), 1g carbohydrate, 2.5g salt	Gluten free • Dairy free	**6**

Grilled Chicken with Pesto Butter

4 skinless chicken breast fillets

75g (3oz) butter, softened

3 tbsp pesto

lemon juice to sprinkle

salt and ground black pepper

tomato salad, parslied new potatoes and lemon wedges to serve

1 Make three or four deep cuts on each side of the chicken breasts. Season well with salt and pepper.

2 Put the butter into a bowl and gradually work in the pesto. Spread half of the pesto butter over the chicken and sprinkle with a little lemon juice.

3 Preheat the grill. Lay the chicken breasts on the grill rack and grill for about 10 minutes. Turn the chicken over, spread with the remaining pesto butter and sprinkle with a little more lemon juice. Grill for about 10 minutes or until cooked through.

4 Serve the chicken on warmed plates, with any pan juices poured over, with tomato salad, potatoes and lemon wedges.

Serves 4	EASY		NUTRITIONAL INFORMATION	
	Preparation Time 10 minutes	**Cooking Time** 20–30 minutes	**Per Serving** 340 calories, 23g fat (of which 12g saturates), trace carbohydrate, 0.6g salt	Gluten free

150ml (¼ pint) bourbon

15g (½oz) soft brown sugar

50ml (2fl oz) clear honey

50ml (2fl oz) tomato ketchup

2 tbsp wholegrain mustard

1 tbsp white wine vinegar

3 garlic cloves, crushed

1 tsp each salt and ground black pepper

4 poussins

chargrilled peppers, tomatoes and onions garnished with flat-leafed parsley to serve

Marinated Poussins

1 Mix the bourbon, sugar, honey, tomato ketchup and mustard together. Stir in the vinegar, garlic, salt and pepper.

2 Put the poussins breast down on a chopping board, then cut through either side of the backbone with poultry shears or a pair of strong sharp scissors and remove it. Open out the poussins, cover them with clingfilm and flatten them slightly by tapping them with the base of a heavy pan. Put the poussins in a shallow glass dish and pour the bourbon marinade over the top, then cover and chill overnight.

3 Preheat the barbecue or grill. Soak eight wooden skewers in water for 20 minutes. Thread the skewers through the legs and breasts of the poussins, keeping the marinade to one side. Cook the poussins for 30 minutes or until cooked through, basting from time to time with the reserved marinade. Serve with the peppers, tomatoes and onions.

EASY		NUTRITIONAL INFORMATION		Serves
Preparation Time 30 minutes, plus overnight marinating	**Cooking Time** 30 minutes	**Per Serving** 508 calories, 30g fat (of which 8g saturates) 10g carbohydrate, 1.6g salt	Gluten free • Dairy free	**4**

3

Meat

Cook's Tip

Salt-baked New Potatoes: toss 550g (1¼lb) par-boiled new potatoes with 2 tbsp olive oil and 1 tbsp sea salt flakes. Cook at 200°C (180°C fan oven) mark 6 for 40 minutes until tender.

Peppercorn Steaks with Aïoli

1 garlic clove, crushed

1 tbsp olive oil

2 tbsp mixed peppercorns, crushed

2 tbsp Dijon mustard

4 x 150g (5oz) sirloin steaks

Salt-baked New Potatoes (see Cook's Tip) and cherry tomatoes to serve

fresh oregano sprigs to garnish

For the aïoli

2 garlic cloves, crushed

200ml (7fl oz) mayonnaise

2 tbsp lemon juice

salt and ground black pepper

1 Mix together the garlic, olive oil, crushed peppercorns and mustard. Spread the mixture on both sides of the steaks and leave to marinate for at least 15 minutes or overnight.

2 To make the aïoli, mix the garlic with the mayonnaise, lemon juice and salt and pepper. Cover and chill until ready to serve.

3 Preheat the barbecue, grill or griddle. Cook the steaks for 3–4 minutes on each side. Allow to rest in a warm place for 5 minutes before serving. Serve with salt-baked new potatoes and cherry tomatoes, and garnish with oregano sprigs. Serve the aïoli in a separate bowl.

	EASY		NUTRITIONAL INFORMATION	
Serves **4**	**Preparation Time** 15 minutes, plus minimum 15 minutes marinating	**Cooking Time** 8 minutes	**Per Serving** 607 calories, 51g fat (of which 9g saturates), 2g carbohydrate, 0.8g salt	Gluten free • Dairy free

Try Something Different

For a more sophisticated burger, replace the cheese and gherkins with thick slices of ripe avocado and use a generous handful of fresh rocket instead of the lettuce.

American-style Hamburgers

1kg (2¼lb) extra-lean minced beef

2 tsp salt

2 tbsp steak seasoning

sunflower oil to brush

6 large soft rolls, halved

6 thin-cut slices havarti or raclette cheese

4 small cocktail gherkins, sliced lengthways

6 tbsp mustard mayonnaise

6 lettuce leaves, such as frisée

4 large vine-ripened tomatoes, sliced thickly

2 large shallots, sliced into thin rings

ground black pepper

1 Put the minced beef into a large bowl and add the salt, steak seasoning and plenty of pepper. Use your hands to mix all the ingredients together thoroughly. Lightly oil the inside of six 10cm (4in) rosti rings and put on a foil-lined baking sheet. Press the meat firmly into the rings, or use your hands to shape the mixture into six even-sized patties. Cover with clingfilm and chill for at least 1 hour.

2 Heat a large griddle pan until it's really hot. Put the rolls, cut sides down, on the griddle and toast.

3 Lightly oil the griddle, ease the burgers out of the moulds and brush with oil. Cook over a medium heat for about 3 minutes, then turn the burgers over carefully. Put a slice of cheese and a few slices of gherkin on top of each and cook for another 3 minutes. While the burgers are cooking, spread the mustard mayonnaise on the toasted side of the rolls. Add the lettuce, tomato and shallots. Put the burgers on top and sandwich with the other half rolls.

EASY		NUTRITIONAL INFORMATION	Serves
Preparation Time 20 minutes, plus 1 hour chilling	**Cooking Time** 10 minutes	**Per Serving** 645 calories, 45g fat (of which 17g saturates), 19g carbohydrate, 2.3g salt	**6**

Teriyaki Beef Sandwiches

700g (1½lb) piece beef sirloin or rump steak, sliced thickly

6 tbsp teriyaki marinade

1 tbsp sesame oil

300ml (½ pint) mayonnaise

4 tsp wasabi paste (see Cook's Tip)

2 ciabatta loaves, split in half lengthways

250g (9oz) baby plum tomatoes, threaded on to metal skewers

olive oil to brush

75g (3oz) fresh rocket

1 small radicchio, shredded

salt and ground black pepper

1 Trim any fat or sinew from the beef and place it in a single layer in a shallow glass dish. Mix together the teriyaki marinade and sesame oil and pour over the meat, turning so it's evenly coated. Cover and leave in the refrigerator for at least 4 hours or overnight, turning occasionally.

2 Mix the mayonnaise with the wasabi, season with salt and pepper, cover and leave in a cool place.

3 Preheat the barbecue or grill. Remove the meat from the marinade and pat dry with kitchen paper. Cook for 15–20 minutes for medium rare and 20–25 minutes for well done, turning frequently to ensure even cooking. Transfer to a board, cover with foil and leave to rest for 10 minutes.

4 Meanwhile, toast the ciabatta halves on the barbecue or grill, wrap in foil and put to one side on the barbecue to keep warm. Brush the tomato skewers with a little olive oil and cook for 1–2 minutes on each side.

5 Slice the beef thinly. Spread two halves of ciabatta liberally with the mayonnaise mixture, top each with rocket and radicchio, slices of warm beef and the tomatoes. Finally, top with more mayonnaise and sandwich together with the remaining ciabatta halves. Cut each loaf into three before serving.

Cook's Tip

Wasabi paste is a Japanese condiment, green in colour and extremely hot – a little goes a long way. It is available from some supermarkets, but if you can't get it, use creamed horseradish instead.

EASY		NUTRITIONAL INFORMATION		Serves
Preparation Time 25 minutes, plus minimum 4 hours marinating	**Cooking Time** 15–25 minutes, plus resting	**Per Serving** 710 calories, 48g fat (of which 9g saturates), 37g carbohydrate, 1.7g salt	Dairy free	**6**

Menu

▼ **Barbecued Lamb Steaks**
▶ **Aubergine, Feta and Tomato Stacks**
   (see page 89)
▶ **Mixed Leaf Salad (see page 101)**
▶ **Apple Bananas with Rum Mascarpone**
   (see page 121)

Barbecued Lamb Steaks

small bunch each of flat-leafed parsley and fresh mint –
or any other herbs – roughly chopped

3 garlic cloves, sliced

1 tbsp Dijon or wholegrain mustard

juice of 2 small lemons

4 tbsp olive oil

4 thick lamb leg steaks

lemon wedges, rocket and crusty bread or
couscous to serve

1 Put the herbs into a small bowl. Add the garlic, mustard, lemon juice and olive oil, and mix well. Put the lamb into a glass dish and spoon over the herb mixture. Cover the dish and marinate for at least 10 minutes.

2 Preheat the barbecue or griddle. Cook the lamb steaks for about 4 minutes on each side (or 5–6 minutes if you like them well done) until golden and crusted. Serve hot, with lemon wedges, rocket and bread or couscous.

Serves 4	EASY		NUTRITIONAL INFORMATION	
	Preparation Time 15 minutes, plus 10 minutes marinating	**Cooking Time** 8–12 minutes	**Per Serving** 322 calories, 23g fat (of which 9g saturates), trace carbohydrate, 0.3g salt	Gluten free • Dairy free

Freezing Tip

Complete the recipe to the end of step 1, place the patties on a tray to freeze, then wrap, label and freeze for up to one month.
To use Thaw at cool room temperature for four hours. Complete the recipe.

Spiced Lamb in Pitta

1 small green pepper, seeded and chopped

½ small onion, chopped

3 garlic cloves

2 tsp ground cumin

3 tbsp olive oil

1 tbsp freshly chopped mint

550g (1¼lb) lean minced lamb

450g (1lb) very ripe tomatoes, chopped

2 tbsp freshly chopped flat-leafed parsley

4 large pitta breads

salt and ground black pepper

Greek yogurt to serve

mint sprigs to garnish

1 Put the chopped pepper and onion in a food processor with the garlic, cumin and olive oil, and pulse to form a coarse paste. Add the chopped mint. Mix together the paste and the minced lamb, season with salt and pepper and shape into 16 patties. Chill for 30 minutes or overnight.

2 Put the tomatoes in a bowl, stir in the parsley and season with salt and pepper.

3 Preheat the barbecue, griddle or grill. Cook the lamb patties for 4–5 minutes on each side. Warm the pitta breads, wrap into a cone and secure with a cocktail stick. Fill each with four lamb patties and spoon on a drizzle of yogurt. Serve with the tomatoes and garnish with mint sprigs.

EASY		NUTRITIONAL INFORMATION	Serves
Preparation Time 20 minutes, plus 30 minutes chilling	**Cooking Time** 8–10 minutes	**Per Serving** 550 calories, 20g fat (of which 9g saturates), 60g carbohydrate, 1.3g salt	**4**

Lamb with Tapenade

6 tbsp olive oil

4 tbsp ready-made tapenade

2 tbsp Pernod or Ricard

2 garlic cloves, crushed

8 loin lamb chops, each about 125g (4oz)

ground black pepper

grilled sliced fennel and courgettes and
lemon halves to serve

1 Mix together the olive oil, tapenade, Pernod or Ricard and the garlic, then rub into the lamb chops and season with black pepper. Leave to marinate for at least 30 minutes or overnight.

2 Preheat the barbecue or griddle. Cook the chops for 4–5 minutes on each side. Serve with lightly grilled fennel slices and courgettes and lemon halves to squeeze over.

Cook's Tips

Tapenade is made from black olives, capers, garlic and olive oil.

The marinade is ideal for other cuts of lamb, such as steaks or fillets, or spread over a boned shoulder or leg.

Serves 4	EASY		NUTRITIONAL INFORMATION	
	Preparation Time 5 minutes, plus minimum 30 minutes marinating	**Cooking Time** 8–10 minutes	**Per Serving** 579 calories, 34g fat (of which 15g saturates), 0g carbohydrate, 0.4g salt	Gluten free • Dairy free

Cook's Tip

Butterflied lamb is a leg of lamb with the bone removed. Most butchers will do this for you.

Butterflied Leg of Lamb

1 leg of lamb, about 2.3kg (5lb) boned

175ml (6fl oz) extra virgin olive oil, plus extra to brush

1 tbsp dried oregano

3 tbsp fresh thyme leaves

2 tbsp freshly chopped flat-leafed parsley

6 garlic cloves, finely chopped

150ml (¼ pint) balsamic vinegar

zest and juice of 2 small really ripe lemons

new potatoes and mixed leaf salad to serve

1 Open out the meat, lay skin side down and trim away any excess fat. Make slits all over it to help the marinade penetrate the flesh. Place the lamb in a large glass dish big enough to take it in a single layer. Whisk the olive oil, herbs, garlic, vinegar, lemon zest and juice together in a small bowl and pour over the meat, rubbing well into the slits. Cover and leave to marinate overnight in the refrigerator.

2 Remove from the refrigerator an hour before barbecuing and put in a cool place. Preheat the barbecue to medium-hot. Lift from the marinade (don't throw it away) and barbecue for 35–40 minutes, turning frequently to ensure even cooking, and basting with the marinade from time to time. The meat should be slightly pink in the centre.

3 Remove from the heat, place on a board and cover loosely with foil. Leave to rest for 10 minutes before carving across the width into long thin slices. Serve with minted new potatoes and a mixed leaf salad.

Serves	EASY		NUTRITIONAL INFORMATION	
8	**Preparation Time** 20 minutes, plus overnight marinating and resting	**Cooking Time** 35–40 minutes	**Per Serving** 509 calories, 32g fat (of which 13g saturates), 1g carbohydrate, 0.3g salt	Gluten free • Dairy free

Lamb, Orange and Apricot Kebabs

700g (1½lb) boned leg of lamb
75g (3oz) ready-to-eat dried apricots
150g (5oz) ready-to-eat dried figs
1 garlic clove, crushed
50g (2oz) spring onions, finely chopped
juice of 2 lemons
6 tbsp Greek yogurt
5 tbsp smooth peanut butter
2 tsp each ground coriander and cumin seeds
1 tsp ground fenugreek
½ tsp chilli powder
3 tbsp olive oil
salt and ground black pepper
225g (8oz) onions
2 large oranges
salad leaves to serve

1 Trim the lamb and cut into large cubes, allowing about three pieces per skewer. Put the apricots and figs in a bowl; add enough water to cover completely, cover and chill.

2 In a large bowl, mix the garlic and spring onions with 8 tbsp lemon juice and all the remaining ingredients apart from the whole onions and oranges. Add the lamb to the marinade and stir to coat well. Cover and chill for at least 6 hours or overnight.

3 Preheat the barbecue and, if using wooden skewers, soak eight in water for 20 minutes. Quarter the onions, then separate the quarters into petals. Thickly slice the oranges. Thread the meat, onions, oranges, apricots and figs on to skewers.

4 Barbecue for 25–30 minutes or until the lamb is pink to the centre. Serve hot, with salad leaves.

EASY		NUTRITIONAL INFORMATION		Serves
Preparation Time 45 minutes, plus marinating	**Cooking Time** 25–30 minutes	**Per Serving** 260 calories, 14g fat (of which 5g saturates), 15g carbohydrate, 0.2g salt	Gluten free	**8**

Moroccan Lamb Kebabs

12 large vine leaves

3 garlic cloves, roughly chopped

1 onion, roughly chopped

½ tsp each ground coriander, ground cumin, sweet paprika and ground ginger

1kg (2¼lb) minced lamb

3 tbsp each freshly chopped mint and coriander

olive oil

salt and ground black pepper

pitta bread, tzatziki, hummus and tomato salad to serve

1 Preheat the barbecue to medium-hot. Soak six long wooden skewers in water for 30 minutes. Rinse the vine leaves and dry on kitchen paper.

2 Put the garlic, onion and spices in a food processor and whiz to form a paste. Add the minced lamb and herbs and pulse again until mixed. Season with salt and pepper. Divide into 12 and, with damp hands, roll into long sausage shapes. Wrap each sausage in a vine leaf and skewer lengthways through the middle, putting two kebabs on each skewer. Brush generously with olive oil and place side by side across the grill rack.

3 Barbecue for 4–5 minutes on each side. Serve with toasted pitta bread, tzatziki, hummus and a tomato salad.

Cook's Tip

Vine leaves preserved in brine are sold in large supermarkets and good delis.

Serves	EASY		NUTRITIONAL INFORMATION	
6	Preparation Time 40 minutes	Cooking Time 8–10 minutes	Per Serving 316 calories, 19g fat (of which 9g saturates), 3g carbohydrate, 0.4g salt	Gluten free • Dairy free

Menu

▼ **Chinese Spare Ribs**
▶ **Vietnamese Rice Salad** (see page 108)
▶ **Mixed Leaf Salad** (see page 101)
▶ **Grilled Coconut Cake** (see page 122)

Chinese Spare Ribs

10 tbsp hoisin sauce

3 tbsp tomato ketchup

1 garlic clove, crushed

2 x 10-bone baby rack of ribs (available from butchers), cut into individual ribs

salt and ground black pepper

1   Put the hoisin sauce, ketchup and garlic in a large shallow dish. Season with salt and pepper and stir everything together until combined.

2   Add the ribs and toss to coat, spooning over the marinade to cover completely. You can either cook the ribs immediately or, if you have time, cover and chill them for 2 hours or overnight.

3   Preheat the barbecue or grill until medium-hot. Alternatively, preheat the oven to 200°C (180°C fan oven) mark 6. Lift the ribs from the marinade and barbecue or grill for 10–12 minutes on each side, or roast in the oven for 45 minutes.

Serves	EASY		NUTRITIONAL INFORMATION	
4	**Preparation Time** 5 minutes, plus 2 hours marinating (optional)	**Cooking Time** 20–45 minutes	**Per Serving** 310 calories, 20g fat (of which 8g saturates), 3g carbohydrate, 0.8g salt	Gluten free • Dairy free

Potato and Sausage Skewers

36 even-sized new potatoes

6 tbsp olive oil, plus extra to brush

12 thick sausages

2 tbsp freshly chopped mint

50g (2oz) freshly grated Parmesan

salt and ground black pepper

rocket to serve

1 Preheat the barbecue. Soak twelve wooden skewers in water for 20 minutes. Boil the potatoes in salted water for about 10 minutes or until almost tender. Drain well and toss with the olive oil, then season with salt and pepper.

2 Cut each sausage into three and thread on to the skewers alternately with the potatoes. Brush with olive oil and barbecue for about 8 minutes, turning from time to time, until the sausages are cooked through and the potatoes begin to char.

3 Meanwhile, put the mint in a bowl, add the Parmesan and stir together until well mixed.

4 When the sausages are cooked, remove the skewers from the barbecue and, while still hot, sprinkle with the mint and Parmesan mixture. Serve with rocket.

EASY		NUTRITIONAL INFORMATION	Serves
Preparation Time 15 minutes	**Cooking Time** 18 minutes	**Per Serving** 789 calories, 52g fat (of which 17g saturates), 58g carbohydrate, 4g salt	**6**

Apricot and Gin-glazed Gammon

4 tbsp gin

6 tbsp apricot jam

4 x 225g (8oz) gammon steaks

75g (3oz) butter, softened

2 tbsp chopped flat-leafed parsley, plus extra sprigs to garnish

50g (2oz) ready-to-eat dried apricots, finely chopped

lemon juice

ground black pepper

Paprika Potatoes (see Cook's Tip) to serve

1 Mix the gin and jam together and cover the gammon steaks with the mixture. Set aside for 10 minutes, or cover and chill overnight. Mix together the butter, parsley, apricots and lemon juice to taste. Season with pepper, cover and chill.

2 Preheat the barbecue or grill. Cook the gammon steaks for 2–3 minutes on each side, then serve immediately, topped with the apricot butter, garnished with parsley sprigs, and with paprika potatoes.

Cook's Tip

Paprika Potatoes: cut 550g (1¼lb) scrubbed potatoes into wedges and cook in a pan of boiling water for 5 minutes. Drain, rinse, then toss in 3 tbsp olive oil, 2 tbsp paprika and plenty of salt and pepper. Barbecue or grill for 10 minutes until golden and cooked through.

EASY		NUTRITIONAL INFORMATION		Serves
Preparation Time 10 minutes, plus 10 minutes marinating	**Cooking Time** 6 minutes	**Per Serving** 710 calories, 43g fat (of which 19g saturates), 20g carbohydrate, 7g salt	Gluten free	**4**

Cook's Tip

Instead of the spring-onion butter, brush four spring onions per person lightly with oil and barbecue or grill for 5 minutes. Squeeze some fresh lime juice on top (saves 30 calories per serving).

2 garlic cloves, crushed

2 small red chillies, finely chopped (including seeds) (see page 32)

1 tsp ground allspice

2 tbsp dark rum

2 tbsp tomato ketchup

4 pork steaks, each weighing about 200g (7oz)

50g (2oz) butter, softened

2 spring onions, thinly sliced

4 corn cobs

salt and ground black pepper

Jamaican-spiced Pork Steaks

1 Mix together the garlic, chillies, allspice, rum and tomato ketchup. Brush all over the pork steaks, cover and chill for at least 30 minutes or overnight.

2 Mix the butter with the spring onions and plenty of black pepper; put to one side or cover and chill overnight.

3 Preheat the barbecue or grill. Cook the corn cobs in salted boiling water for 2 minutes. Drain well, then barbecue or grill until cooked and beginning to char – about 4–5 minutes. Barbecue or grill the pork for about 5 minutes on each side until cooked through. Serve with the corn, smothered in spring-onion butter.

Serves 4	EASY		NUTRITIONAL INFORMATION	
	Preparation Time 20 minutes, plus minimum 30 minutes marinating	**Cooking Time** 10 minutes	**Per Serving** 355 calories, 18g fat (of which 9g saturates), trace carbohydrate, 0.5g salt	Gluten free

Try Something Different

You can use any sturdy fresh aromatic herb: oregano or rosemary would make good alternatives to thyme.

Herb Sausages with Mustard Dip

12 sausages

12 rashers smoked streaky bacon

2 tbsp fresh thyme leaves

4 tbsp wholegrain mustard

8 tbsp mayonnaise

250g (9oz) small tomatoes

salt and ground black pepper

1 Put the sausages in a pan of boiling water, bring back to the boil and simmer gently for 3 minutes, then drain and leave to cool. Wrap each cold sausage in a rasher of stretched bacon sprinkled with thyme leaves (so the thyme sits next to the sausage) and spear with a wet cocktail stick to secure.

2 Mix together the mustard and mayonnaise and season to taste with salt and pepper.

3 Preheat the barbecue or grill. Cook the sausages for 7–8 minutes until well browned. Barbecue or grill the tomatoes for about 1 minute or until the skins begin to blister and burst.

4 Remove the cocktail sticks from the sausages and serve with the mustard dip and grilled tomatoes.

EASY		NUTRITIONAL INFORMATION		Serves
Preparation Time 10 minutes	**Cooking Time** 11 minutes	**Per Serving** 836 calories, 76g fat (of which 23g saturates), 16g carbohydrate, 5g salt	Dairy free	**4**

4

Vegetables

Mediterranean Kebabs

1 large courgette, cut into chunks

1 red pepper, seeded and cut into chunks

12 cherry tomatoes

125g (4oz) halloumi cheese, cubed

100g (3½oz) natural yogurt

1 tsp ground cumin

2 tbsp olive oil

squeeze of lemon

1 lemon, cut into eight wedges

couscous tossed with freshly chopped flat-leafed parsley to serve

1 Preheat the barbecue or grill. Soak eight wooden skewers in water for 20 minutes. Put the courgette into a large bowl with the red pepper, cherry tomatoes and halloumi cheese. Add the yogurt, cumin, olive oil and a squeeze of lemon and mix.

2 Push a lemon wedge on to each skewer, then divide the vegetables and cheese among the skewers. Grill the kebabs, turning regularly, for 8–10 minutes until the vegetables are tender and the halloumi is nicely charred. Serve with couscous.

Serves 4	EASY		NUTRITIONAL INFORMATION	
	Preparation Time 15 minutes	Cooking Time 8–10 minutes	Per Serving 164 calories, 13g fat (of which 5g saturates), 7g carbohydrate, 1.1g salt	Vegetarian Gluten free

Cook's Tip

Yogurt Sauce: mix together 225g (8oz) Greek yogurt, 1 crushed garlic clove and 2 tbsp freshly chopped coriander. Season with salt and pepper. Chill until ready to serve.

Spicy Vegetable Kebabs

12 baby onions

12 new potatoes

12 button mushrooms

2 courgettes

2 garlic cloves, crushed

1 tsp each ground coriander and turmeric

½ tsp ground cumin

1 tbsp sun-dried tomato paste

1 tsp chilli sauce

juice of ½ lemon

4 tbsp olive oil

275g (10oz) smoked tofu, cut into 2.5cm (1in) cubes

salt and ground black pepper

Yogurt Sauce (see Cook's Tip) and lemon wedges to serve

1 Blanch the baby onions in a pan of boiling salted water for 3 minutes; drain, refresh in cold water and peel away the skins. Put the potatoes into a pan of cold salted water, bring to the boil and parboil for 8 minutes; drain and refresh under cold water. Blanch the button mushrooms in boiling water for 1 minute; drain and refresh under cold water. Cut each courgette into six chunky slices and blanch for 1 minute; drain and refresh.

2 Mix the garlic, spices, tomato paste, chilli sauce, lemon juice, olive oil, salt and pepper together in a shallow dish. Add the well-drained vegetables and tofu and toss to coat. Cover and chill for several hours or overnight.

3 Preheat the barbecue or grill. Soak six wooden skewers in water for 20 minutes. Thread the vegetables and tofu on to the skewers. Cook the kebabs for 8–10 minutes until the vegetables are charred and tender, turning frequently and basting with the marinade. Serve with Yogurt Sauce and lemon wedges.

EASY		NUTRITIONAL INFORMATION		Serves
Preparation Time 30 minutes, plus marinating	**Cooking Time** 25 minutes	**Per Serving** 247 calories, 14g fat (of which 3g saturates), 22g carbohydrate, 0.1g salt	Vegetarian Gluten free	**6**

Grilled Vegetables with Walnut Sauce

2 large carrots, peeled

1 fennel bulb

225g (8oz) sweet potatoes

225g (8oz) Jerusalem artichokes, scrubbed

225g (8oz) thick asparagus spears

8 baby leeks

4–6 tbsp olive oil

salt and ground black pepper

For the walnut sauce

50g (2oz) day-old bread, crusts removed

75g (3oz) walnuts, toasted

2 garlic cloves, chopped

1 tbsp red wine vinegar

2 tbsp chopped parsley

90ml (3fl oz) olive oil

50ml (2fl oz) walnut oil

1 First make the walnut sauce. Crumble the bread into a bowl, add 2 tbsp water, then squeeze dry. Put the bread into a food processor with the toasted walnuts, garlic, wine vinegar and parsley; blend until fairly smooth. Add the olive and walnut oils and process briefly to form a thick sauce. Season with salt and pepper and transfer to a serving dish.

2 Preheat the grill to medium-high. Prepare the vegetables. Cut the carrots into 5mm (¼in) slices; thinly slice the fennel lengthways; peel and thinly slice the sweet potatoes; thinly slice the Jerusalem artichokes. Trim the asparagus and leeks, but leave whole.

3 Baste the vegetables with olive oil and grill in batches, turning once, for 2–6 minutes on each side until charred and tender (see Cook's Tip); keep warm in a low oven while grilling the rest.

4 Transfer all the grilled vegetables to a warmed serving plate and season with a little salt and pepper. Serve accompanied by the walnut sauce.

Cook's Tip

The root vegetables take longest to cook through, while the asparagus and leeks only need a short time under the grill.

EASY		NUTRITIONAL INFORMATION		Serves
Preparation Time 25 minutes	**Cooking Time** 15–20 minutes	**Per Serving** 598 calories, 48g fat (of which 6g saturates), 35g carbohydrate, 0.3g salt	Vegetarian Dairy free	4

Grilled Mediterranean Vegetables

6 garlic cloves

2 red peppers, seeded and cut into thick strips

4 courgettes, quartered lengthways and cut into sticks

2 aubergines, cut into sticks the same size as the courgettes

2 small red onions, cut into wedges

100ml (3½fl oz) olive oil

salt and ground black pepper

1 Blanch the whole cloves of garlic in boiling water for 5 minutes.

2 Put all the vegetables into a shallow glass dish and pour the olive oil over. Season with salt and pepper. Cover and chill for up to six hours.

3 Preheat the barbecue, griddle or grill. Lay the vegetables in a single layer on the grill rack (you may need to do two batches) and cook for about 10 minutes, turning once or twice, until they are slightly charred. Serve hot or cold.

Serves 4	EASY		NUTRITIONAL INFORMATION	
	Preparation Time 10 minutes, plus 6 hours chilling	**Cooking Time** 20 minutes	**Per Serving** 234 calories, 18g fat (of which 3g saturates), 16g carbohydrate, trace salt	Vegetarian Gluten free • Dairy free

Try Something Different

Replace the feta with sliced mozzarella, or smoked mozzarella. Mix some olive oil with the crushed garlic, brush over the mozzarella and stack up in step 3.

Aubergine, Feta and Tomato Stacks

200g (7oz) feta cheese, crumbled

2 tbsp olive oil, plus extra to brush

1 garlic clove, crushed, plus 1 garlic clove for rubbing

2 plump aubergines, cut into 1cm (½ in) thick slices

a handful of fresh basil leaves, torn

3 large vine-ripened tomatoes, each sliced into four

salt and ground black pepper

rocket and toasted ciabatta to serve

1 Preheat the barbecue or grill. Put the feta into a bowl, stir in the olive oil and garlic, season with salt and pepper and set aside.

2 Brush each aubergine slice with a little olive oil and barbecue or grill for about 6 minutes, turning occasionally until softened and golden. Remove from the heat.

3 Sprinkle a little of the feta mixture on to six of the aubergine slices, put some torn basil leaves on top, then a slice of tomato. Season well. Repeat with the feta mixture, basil leaves, aubergine and tomato. Finish with an aubergine slice and press down firmly.

4 Secure each stack with a cocktail stick. Either use a hinged grill rack, well oiled, or wrap the stacks in foil and barbecue for 2–3 minutes on each side. Serve with rocket leaves and toasted ciabatta rubbed with a garlic clove.

EASY		NUTRITIONAL INFORMATION		Serves
Preparation Time 10 minutes	**Cooking Time** 12 minutes	**Per Serving** 138 calories, 11g fat (of which 5g saturates), 4g carbohydrate, 1.2g salt	Vegetarian Gluten free	**6**

Try Something Different

Instead of the steak seasoning, lightly toast 2 tsp coriander seeds, roughly crush and stir into the melted butter before brushing on to the squash. When cooked, toss with fresh coriander leaves.

Spicy Squash Quarters

2 small butternut squash, quartered and seeds discarded
coarse sea salt to sprinkle
75g (3oz) butter, melted
4 tsp peppered steak seasoning
wild rocket to serve

1 Preheat the barbecue to medium-hot. Sprinkle the squash with sea salt, brush with butter and sprinkle the steak seasoning over.

2 Cook the squash for 20–30 minutes until tender, turning occasionally. Serve hot, with wild rocket.

Serves	EASY		NUTRITIONAL INFORMATION	
8	**Preparation Time** 10 minutes	**Cooking Time** 20–30 minutes	**Per Serving** 97 calories, 8g fat (of which 5g saturates), 4g carbohydrate, 0.1g salt	Vegetarian Gluten free

Menu

▶ American-style Hamburgers (see page 65)
▼ Red Onions with Rosemary Dressing
▶ Cranberry Cooler (see page 126)

Red Onions with Rosemary Dressing

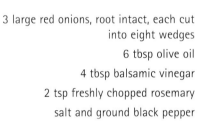

3 large red onions, root intact, each cut into eight wedges
6 tbsp olive oil
4 tbsp balsamic vinegar
2 tsp freshly chopped rosemary
salt and ground black pepper

1 Preheat the barbecue. Soak eight wooden skewers in water for 20 minutes. Thread the onion wedges on to the skewers. Brush with about 3 tbsp olive oil, then season well with salt and pepper.

2 Barbecue the onion kebabs for 30–35 minutes, turning from time to time and brushing with oil when necessary, until tender and lightly charred.

3 To make the dressing, mix together the balsamic vinegar, remaining olive oil and the rosemary. Drizzle the rosemary dressing over the cooked onions and serve.

EASY		NUTRITIONAL INFORMATION		Serves
Preparation Time 20 minutes	**Cooking Time** 30–35 minutes	**Per Serving** 91 calories, 6g fat (of which trace saturates), 9g carbohydrate, trace salt	Vegetarian Gluten free • Dairy free	**8**

Grilled Sweet Potatoes with Feta and Olives

1 large sweet potato, weighing about 500g (1lb 2oz)

4 tbsp olive oil, plus extra to brush

200g (7oz) feta cheese

2 tsp dried herbes de Provence

50g (2oz) pitted black olives, chopped

1 garlic clove, crushed

salt and ground black pepper

flat-leafed parsley sprigs to garnish

1 Preheat the barbecue or griddle. Peel the sweet potato and cut lengthways into eight wedges. Put them in a pan of boiling water, bring back to the boil, simmer for 3 minutes, then drain and refresh in cold water. Drain, dry well on kitchen paper, then brush lightly with olive oil. Season with salt and pepper, then barbecue or grill for 10–15 minutes until well browned and cooked through.

2 Meanwhile, mash the cheese, herbs, olives, garlic and 4 tbsp olive oil together. Serve the sweet potato with the feta cheese mixture, garnished with flat-leafed parsley.

Cook's Tip

Herbes de Provence, an aromatic dried mixture made up of rosemary, thyme, basil, bay and savory, is a wonderful complement to barbecued or grilled food.

For an authentic Mediterranean flavour, mix herbes de Provence with olive oil and brush over chicken or lamb, then rub with coarse salt before grilling.

Serves 4	EASY		NUTRITIONAL INFORMATION	
	Preparation Time 15 minutes	**Cooking Time** 15–20 minutes	**Per Serving** 324 calories, 23g fat (of which 9g saturates), 21g carbohydrate, 2.5g salt	Vegetarian Gluten free

Cook's Tip

Skewering the potatoes helps them to cook more quickly and makes them easier to handle on a barbecue. Using rosemary stalks adds a wonderful flavour.

Roasted Rosemary Potatoes

750g (1lb 11oz) new potatoes
3 tbsp olive oil
8 rosemary stalks, each about 18cm (7in) long
salt and ground black pepper

1 Preheat the barbecue or grill. Cook the potatoes, unpeeled, in boiling salted water for 10 minutes or until nearly tender. Drain, cool a little, then toss in the olive oil. Season well. Strip most of the leaves from the rosemary stalks, leaving a few at the tip; set the stripped leaves to one side.

2 Thread the potatoes on to the rosemary stalks, place on the barbecue or grill and scatter with the leaves. Cook for 10–15 minutes, turning from time to time, until tender and lightly charred.

Serves 8	EASY		NUTRITIONAL INFORMATION	
	Preparation Time 10 minutes	**Cooking Time** 20–25 minutes	**Per Serving** 102 calories, 4g fat (of which 1g saturates), 15g carbohydrate, trace salt	Vegetarian Gluten free • Dairy free

Try Something Different

Mix the olive oil with a good pinch of dried chilli flakes and a small handful of chopped fresh rosemary leaves.
Use a mixture of yellow and green courgettes if you like.

Charred Courgettes

4 courgettes, halved lengthways

olive oil to brush

coarse sea salt to sprinkle

1 Preheat the barbecue or griddle. Score a criss-cross pattern on the fleshy side of the courgettes. Brush lightly with olive oil and sprinkle with sea salt.

2 Cook the courgettes on the barbecue or griddle for 10 minutes or until just tender, turning occasionally.

EASY		NUTRITIONAL INFORMATION		Serves
Preparation Time 5 minutes	**Cooking Time** 10 minutes	**Per Serving** 36 calories, 2g fat (of which trace saturates), 2g carbohydrate, 0g salt	Vegetarian Gluten free • Dairy free	**4**

5

Salads and Breads

Melon, Mango and Cucumber Salad with Wasabi Dressing

½ cucumber, halved lengthways and seeded

1 Charentais melon, halved and seeded

1 mango, peeled and stoned

freshly chopped flat-leafed parsley and lime wedges to serve

For the wasabi dressing

3 tsp soy sauce

1 tbsp dry sherry

1 tbsp rice wine vinegar or white wine vinegar

¼ tsp wasabi paste (see page 67) or finely chopped green chilli (see page 32)

1 Cut the cucumber into slim diagonal slices. Cut the rind off the melon and cut the flesh into similar-sized pieces to the cucumber. Cut the mango flesh into similar-sized lengths. Mix the cucumber, melon and mango in a large bowl.

2 To make the wasabi dressing, in a small bowl, whisk together the soy sauce, sherry, vinegar and wasabi paste or chilli, then toss with the salad. Sprinkle with chopped flat-leafed parsley, and serve with lime wedges.

Get Ahead

Complete the recipe, store in an airtight container and keep chilled for up to one day.

Serves 6	EASY		NUTRITIONAL INFORMATION	
	Preparation Time 15 minutes, plus chilling		**Per Serving** 62 calories, trace fat (of which 0g saturates), 14g carbohydrate, 1.5g salt	Vegetarian Gluten free • Dairy free

Asparagus with Lemon Dressing

250g (9oz) fine-stemmed asparagus, ends trimmed

salt and ground black pepper

For the lemon dressing

finely grated zest of ½ lemon

2 tbsp lemon juice

3 tbsp extra virgin olive oil

a pinch of golden caster sugar

1 To make the lemon dressing, put the lemon zest into a screwtopped jar, add the lemon juice, oil and sugar, secure the lid tightly, then shake well to mix.

2 Half-fill a frying pan with boiling salted water. Add the asparagus, then cover and simmer for 5 minutes or until just tender.

3 Remove the asparagus with a large draining spoon. If serving the asparagus cold, plunge it into a large bowl of iced water (this will help to keep its bright green colour), then drain.

4 To serve, arrange the asparagus in a shallow bowl, season with salt and pepper and drizzle with the dressing.

Serves 4	EASY		NUTRITIONAL INFORMATION	
	Preparation Time 15 minutes	**Cooking Time** 5 minutes	**Per Serving** 73 calories, 7g fat (of which 1g saturates), 1g carbohydrate, 0g salt	Vegetarian Gluten free • Dairy free

Try Something Different

Blue Cheese Dressing: crumble 50g (2oz) blue cheese into a food processor, together with 2 tbsp low-fat natural yogurt, 1 tbsp white wine vinegar and 5 tbsp olive oil. Whiz for 1 minute until smooth. Season with salt and pepper.
Balsamic Dressing: put 2 tbsp balsamic vinegar into a screwtopped jar with 4 tbsp extra virgin olive oil, salt and pepper. Secure the lid tightly and shake vigorously to mix.

3 round lettuce hearts, roughly shredded

100g (3½oz) watercress

2 ripe avocados, roughly chopped

1 box salad cress, chopped

100g (3½oz) sugarsnap peas, roughly sliced

Mixed Leaf Salad

For the vinaigrette dressing

1 tbsp white wine vinegar

4 tbsp olive oil

salt and ground black pepper

1 Put the lettuce hearts into a bowl and add the watercress, avocados, salad cress and sugarsnap peas.

2 To make the vinaigrette dressing, put all the ingredients into a screwtopped jar, secure the lid tightly and shake vigorously to mix. Pour the dressing over the salad and toss to mix; serve immediately.

EASY	NUTRITIONAL INFORMATION		Serves
Preparation Time 15 minutes	**Per Serving** 144 calories, 12g fat (of which 2g saturates), 4g carbohydrate, 0.2g salt	Vegetarian Gluten free • Dairy free	**8**

Summer Vegetable Salad

600g (1lb 5oz) mixed green vegetables, such as French beans, peas, sugarsnap peas, asparagus and broccoli

¼ small cucumber, halved lengthways, seeded and sliced

2 tbsp freshly chopped flat-leafed parsley

salt

For the mustard dressing

1 tbsp white wine or sherry vinegar

1 tsp English mustard powder

3 tbsp extra virgin olive oil

1 Cook the beans in a large pan of boiling salted water for 3 minutes, then add all the other vegetables. Bring the water back to the boil and cook for a further 3–4 minutes. Drain well and put immediately into a bowl of ice-cold water.

2 Whisk the dressing ingredients together in a small bowl.

3 To serve, drain the vegetables, then toss in the dressing with the cucumber and parsley.

Serves 4	EASY		NUTRITIONAL INFORMATION	
	Preparation Time 5 minutes	**Cooking Time** 10 minutes	**Per Serving** 54 calories, 4g fat (of which 1g saturates), 3g carbohydrate, 0g salt	Vegetarian Gluten free • Dairy free

Try Something Different

Instead of flageolet beans, use cannellini, haricot or borlotti beans.

Simple Bean Salad

2 tbsp olive oil

2 garlic cloves, sliced

2 x 400g cans flageolet beans, drained and rinsed

extra virgin olive oil to drizzle

2 tbsp fresh pesto sauce

lemon juice to taste

a small handful of basil leaves, bruised

salt and ground black pepper

1 Put the olive oil into a small pan and fry the garlic until golden. Stir in the flageolet beans, then leave to marinate in the oil for 10–15 minutes.

2 When ready to serve, drizzle a little extra virgin olive oil over the beans until generously coated. Add the pesto sauce and lemon juice to taste and season with salt and pepper, then stir in the basil leaves.

EASY		NUTRITIONAL INFORMATION		Serves
Preparation Time 5 minutes, plus 10–15 minutes marinating	**Cooking Time** 5 minutes	**Per Serving** 208 calories, 10g fat (of which 2g saturates), 21g carbohydrate, 1.2g salt	Vegetarian Gluten free	**6**

Warm Broad Bean and Feta Salad

225g (8oz) broad beans – if using fresh beans you will need to start with 700g (1½lb) pods

100g (3½oz) feta cheese, chopped

2 tbsp freshly chopped mint

2 tbsp extra virgin olive oil

a squeeze of lemon juice

salt and ground black pepper

lemon wedges to serve

1 Cook the beans in boiling salted water for 3–5 minutes until tender. Drain, then plunge into cold water and drain again.

2 Tip the beans into a bowl, add the feta, mint and olive oil and a squeeze of lemon juice. Season well and toss together. Serve with lemon wedges.

Menu

▶ Lemon Tuna (see page 38)
▲ Warm Broad Bean and Feta Salad
▶ Roasted Rosemary Potatoes (see page 94)
▶ Sweet Kebabs (see page 120)

EASY		NUTRITIONAL INFORMATION		Serves
Preparation Time 15 minutes	**Cooking Time** 3–5 minutes	**Per Serving** 321 calories, 22g fat (of which 8g saturates), 15g carbohydrate, 1.8g salt	Vegetarian Gluten free	2

Creamy Potato Salad

550g (1¼lb) new potatoes

6 tbsp mayonnaise

2 tbsp crème fraîche

2 tbsp white wine vinegar

2 shallots, finely chopped

4 tbsp chopped gherkins

2 tbsp olive oil

salt and ground black pepper

1 Cook the potatoes in a pan of boiling salted water for 15–20 minutes until tender. Drain, leave to cool slightly, then chop.

2 Mix together the mayonnaise, crème fraîche, vinegar, shallots, gherkins and olive oil. Season with salt and pepper and mix with the potatoes. Leave to cool, then chill until ready to serve.

Serves 4	EASY		NUTRITIONAL INFORMATION	
	Preparation Time 10 minutes	**Cooking Time** 15–20 minutes	**Per Serving** 335 calories, 26g fat (of which 6g saturates), 24g carbohydrate, 0.3g salt	Vegetarian Gluten free

Red Pepper Pasta Salad

2 red peppers

6 tbsp olive oil

1 garlic clove, crushed

2 tsp Dijon mustard

2 tbsp balsamic vinegar

350g (12oz) cooked drained pasta

3 tbsp freshly chopped herbs, such as parsley, thyme or basil

salt and ground black pepper

1 Place the peppers on an oiled barbecue grill rack or under a preheated grill. Alternatively, using tongs, hold the peppers over the gas flame on your hob. Turn frequently, until the skin begins to char all over. Put in a bowl, cover and leave to cool (the steam will help to loosen the skin). Peel off the skin, scrape out the seeds and cut into strips.

2 Mix together the olive oil, garlic, mustard and balsamic vinegar and stir into the freshly cooked pasta. Season with salt and pepper and leave to cool. Add the pepper strips and serve sprinkled with the herbs.

EASY		NUTRITIONAL INFORMATION		Serves
Preparation Time 5 minutes	**Cooking Time** 20 minutes	**Per Serving** 275 calories, 18g fat (of which 3g saturates), 26g carbohydrate, 0.3g salt	Vegetarian Dairy free	**4**

Vietnamese Rice Salad

225g (8oz) mixed basmati and wild rice

1 large carrot, coarsely grated

1 large courgette, coarsely grated

1 red onion, finely sliced

4 tbsp roasted salted peanuts, lightly chopped

20g (³⁄₄oz) each fresh coriander, mint and basil, roughly chopped

100g (3½oz) wild rocket

For the Vietnamese dressing

2 tbsp light muscovado sugar

juice of 2 limes

4 tbsp fish sauce

6 tbsp rice wine vinegar or white wine vinegar

2 tbsp sunflower oil

1 Put the rice in a pan with 500ml (18fl oz) water. Cover, bring to the boil and cook for 20 minutes until the rice is just cooked. Tip on to a plastic tray, spread out and leave to cool.

2 Meanwhile, make the dressing. Put the sugar in a small pan and heat gently until it just begins to melt. Add the lime juice, fish sauce and vinegar. Stir over a low heat to dissolve the sugar. Take off the heat and add the oil. Stir into the rice with the carrot, courgette and onion.

3 Spoon the salad into a large bowl and top with peanuts, herbs and rocket. Cover and keep chilled.

Get Ahead

Complete the recipe to the end of step 2 and store in an airtight container in the refrigerator for up to two days. **To use** Complete the recipe.

Serves 6	EASY		NUTRITIONAL INFORMATION	
	Preparation Time 10 minutes	**Cooking Time** 20 minutes	**Per Serving** 294 calories, 14g fat (of which 2g saturates), 38g carbohydrate, 0.6g salt	Gluten free • Dairy free

Menu

▼ **Summer Couscous**
▶ **Prawn and Fish Kebabs** (see page 35)
▶ **Barbecue Banoffee** (see page 117)
▶ **Sangria** (see page 123)

Summer Couscous

175g (6oz) baby plum tomatoes, halved
2 small aubergines, thickly sliced
2 large yellow peppers, seeded and roughly chopped
2 red onions, cut into thin wedges
2 fat garlic cloves, crushed
5 tbsp olive oil
250g (9oz) couscous
400g can chopped tomatoes
2 tbsp harissa paste
25g (1oz) toasted pumpkin seeds (optional)
1 large bunch coriander, roughly chopped
salt and ground black pepper

1 Preheat the oven to 230°C (210°C fan oven) mark 8. Put the vegetables and garlic into a large roasting tin, drizzle over 3 tbsp olive oil and season with salt and pepper. Toss to coat. Roast for 20 minutes or until tender.

2 Meanwhile, put the couscous into a separate roasting tin and add 300ml (½ pint) cold water. Leave to soak for 5 minutes. Stir in the tomatoes and harissa, and drizzle with the remaining oil. Pop in the oven next to the vegetables for 4–5 minutes to warm through.

3 Stir the pumpkin seeds, if you like, and the coriander into the couscous and season. Add the vegetables and stir through.

Serves 4	EASY		NUTRITIONAL INFORMATION	
	Preparation Time 10 minutes	**Cooking Time** 20 minutes	**Per Serving** 405 calories, 21g fat (of which 3g saturates), 49g carbohydrate, 0g salt	Vegetarian Dairy free

Cook's Tip

Use dried polenta grains for this recipe.

oil to grease

125g (4oz) plain flour

175g (6oz) polenta or cornmeal

1 tbsp baking powder

1 tbsp caster sugar

½ tsp salt

300ml (½ pint) buttermilk, or equal quantities of natural yogurt and milk, mixed together

2 medium eggs

4 tbsp extra virgin olive oil

Cornbread

1 Preheat the oven to 200°C (180°C fan oven) mark 6. Generously grease a 20.5cm (8in) square shallow tin.

2 Put the flour into a large bowl, then add the polenta or cornmeal, the baking powder, sugar and salt. Make a well in the centre and pour in the buttermilk or yogurt and milk mixture. Add the eggs and olive oil, then stir together until evenly mixed.

3 Pour into the tin and bake for 25–30 minutes until firm to the touch. Insert a skewer into the centre – if it comes out clean, the cornbread is done.

4 Leave the cornbread to rest in the tin for 5 minutes, then turn out and cut into chunky triangles. Serve warm with butter.

EASY		NUTRITIONAL INFORMATION		Serves
Preparation Time 5 minutes	**Cooking Time** 25–30 minutes	**Per Serving** 229 calories, 8g fat (of which 1g saturates), 33g carbohydrate, 1.3g salt	Vegetarian	**8**

Freezing Tip

Wrap and freeze after sprinkling with salt at step 4.
To use Bake the dough from frozen at 200°C (180°C fan oven) mark 6 for 35–40 minutes until cooked through.

Black Olive Bread

2 tsp traditional dried yeast

500g (1lb 2oz) strong white bread flour, plus extra to dust

2 tsp coarse salt, plus extra to sprinkle

6 tbsp extra virgin olive oil, plus extra to grease

100g (3½oz) black olives, pitted and chopped

1 Put 150ml (¼ pint) hand-hot water into a jug, stir in the yeast and leave for 10 minutes or until foamy. Put the flour into a bowl or a food processor, then add the salt, yeast mix, 200ml (7fl oz) warm water and 2 tbsp olive oil. Mix using a wooden spoon or the dough hook for 2–3 minutes to make a soft smooth dough. Put the dough in a lightly oiled bowl; cover with oiled clingfilm and leave in a warm place for 45 minutes or until doubled in size. Punch the dough to knock out the air, then knead on a lightly floured worksurface for 1 minute. Add the olives and knead until combined. Divide in half, shape into rectangles and put into two greased tins, each about 25.5 x 15cm (10 x 6in). Cover with clingfilm and leave in a warm place for 1 hour or until the dough is puffy.

2 Preheat the oven to 200°C (180°C fan oven) mark 6. Press your finger into the dough 12 times, drizzle over 2 tbsp oil and sprinkle with salt. Bake for 30–35 minutes until golden. Drizzle with the remaining oil. Slice and serve warm.

Makes 2 loaves	EASY		NUTRITIONAL INFORMATION	
	Preparation Time 40 minutes, plus 2 hours rising	**Cooking Time** 30–35 minutes	**Per loaf** 600 calories, 21g fat (of which 3g saturates), 97g carbohydrate, 3.8g salt	Vegetarian Dairy free

Griddled Garlic Bread

1 large crusty loaf
175g (6oz) butter, cubed
3 garlic cloves, crushed
a bunch of stiff-stemmed fresh thyme sprigs
salt and ground black pepper

1 Cut the bread into 2cm (¾in) thick slices.

2 Put the butter and garlic in a small metal or heatproof dish (a tin mug is ideal) and sit it on the barbecue grill. Leave to melt. Season with salt and pepper.

3 Dip the thyme into the melted butter and brush one side of each slice of bread. Put the slices, buttered side down, on the barbecue grill. Cook for 1–2 minutes until crisp and golden. Brush the uppermost sides with the remaining butter, turn over and cook the other side. Serve immediately.

EASY		NUTRITIONAL INFORMATION		Serves
Preparation Time 5 minutes	**Cooking Time** 5–6 minutes	**Per Serving** 400 calories, 20g fat (of which 11g saturates), 50g carbohydrate, 1.6g salt	Vegetarian	**8**

6

Desserts and Drinks

Barbecued Figs with Marsala

12 large ripe figs
melted butter to brush
1 cinnamon stick, roughly broken
6 tbsp clear Greek honey
6 tbsp Marsala
crème fraîche to serve

1 Make a small slit in each fig, three-quarters of the way through. Take two sheets of foil large enough to hold the figs in one layer. With the shiny side uppermost, lay one piece on top of the other and brush the top piece all over with the melted butter.

2 Stand the figs in the middle of the foil and scatter over the broken cinnamon stick. Bring the sides of the foil together loosely and pour in the honey and Marsala. Scrunch the edges of the foil together so that the figs are loosely enclosed.

3 Put the foil parcel on the barbecue and cook for 10–15 minutes.

4 Just before serving, open up the foil slightly at the top and barbecue for a further 2–3 minutes to allow the juices to reduce and become syrupy. Serve the figs immediately with a large dollop of crème fraîche and the syrupy juices spooned over.

Serves 4	EASY		NUTRITIONAL INFORMATION	
	Preparation Time 10 minutes	Cooking Time 20 minutes	Per Serving 106 calories, trace fat, 22g carbohydrate, 0g salt	Vegetarian Gluten free

Barbecue Banoffee

4 bananas, peeled

75g (3oz) vanilla fudge, roughly chopped

butter to grease

4 tbsp rum or brandy

thick cream or ice cream to serve

1 Make a long slit in each banana. Divide the fudge among the bananas, then place the bananas on four large squares of buttered foil. Spoon 1 tbsp rum or brandy over each banana and scrunch the edges of the foil together to make loose parcels.

2 Put the foil parcels on the barbecue or under a hot grill and cook for 4–5 minutes. Serve hot, with thick cream or vanilla ice cream.

EASY		NUTRITIONAL INFORMATION		Serves
Preparation Time 5 minutes	**Cooking Time** 4–5 minutes	**Per Serving** 210 calories, 3g fat (of which 2g saturates), 38g carbohydrate, 0.1g salt	Vegetarian Gluten free	**4**

Warm Plum Brioche Toasts

8 plums, halved and stoned

butter to grease

2 tbsp fruit liqueur, such as Kirsch

2 tbsp golden caster sugar

1 vanilla pod, split

grilled brioche and mascarpone to serve

1 Put the halved plums on a large piece of buttered foil. Sprinkle over the fruit liqueur and sugar and add the split vanilla pod. Scrunch the edges of the foil together to make a loose parcel.

2 Put the foil parcel on the barbecue and cook for 10 minutes. Serve hot, with lightly grilled brioche slices and mascarpone cheese.

EASY		NUTRITIONAL INFORMATION		Serves
Preparation Time 10 minutes	**Cooking Time** 10 minutes	**Per Serving** 46 calories, trace fat, 10g carbohydrate, 0g salt	Vegetarian	**8**

Sweet Kebabs

chocolate brownie, about 10 x 5cm (4 x 2in), cut into eight chunks

8 large strawberriees

whipped cream to serve

1 Spear alternate chunks of chocolate brownie and strawberries on to skewers; barbecue or grill for 3 minutes, turning occasionally. Serve with whipped cream.

Serves 4	EASY		NUTRITIONAL INFORMATION	
	Preparation Time 5 minutes	**Cooking Time** 3 minutes	**Per Serving** 521 calories, 23g fat (of which 12g saturates), 77g carbohydrate, 0.3g salt	Vegetarian

Cook's Tips

Apple bananas are a dwarf variety of banana with a delicate apple flavour. They are sold in supermarkets, sometimes in the exotics section.
Small bananas work just as well.

Apple Bananas with Rum Mascarpone

250g (9oz) mascarpone, chilled

2–3 tsp light muscovado sugar

2–3 tbsp dark rum

12 apple bananas (see Cook's Tips)

75g (3oz) plain chocolate, chopped

1 Spoon the mascarpone into a bowl and stir in the sugar and rum. Cover and set aside in a cool place.

2 Barbecue the unpeeled bananas over medium-hot coals for 8–10 minutes, turning frequently until tender and blackened.

3 Split the bananas open, sprinkle a little chocolate inside each and top with the rum mascarpone. Sprinkle over the remaining chocolate before serving.

EASY		NUTRITIONAL INFORMATION		Serves
Preparation Time 10 minutes	**Cooking Time** 8–10 minutes	**Per Serving** 260 calories, 10g fat (of which 6g saturates), 35g carbohydrate, 0g salt	Vegetarian Gluten free	**6**

Try Something Different

Passion Fruit Sauce: scoop the pulp from 8 ripe passion fruit into a food processor and briefly whiz to loosen the seeds and pulp. Transfer to a small pan with 1 tbsp sugar and 2 tbsp coconut rum liqueur, such as Malibu, and simmer for 2–3 minutes, until syrupy. Cool. Drizzle over the grilled cake and serve with fresh tropical fruits.

Grilled Coconut Cake

4 thick slices coconut or Madeira cake

icing sugar to dust

Greek yogurt or crème fraîche and fresh fruit to serve

1 Grill the cake until lightly charred on both sides. Dust with icing sugar and serve with thick Greek yogurt and fresh fruit, cut into bite-size pieces.

Serves 4	EASY		NUTRITIONAL INFORMATION	
	Preparation Time 5 minutes	**Cooking Time** 5 minutes	**Per Serving** 434 calories, 24g fat (of which 0g saturates), 51g carbohydrate, 1g salt	Vegetarian

1 lemon, sliced

1 orange, sliced

1 lime, sliced

75cl bottle red wine

50ml (2fl oz) Spanish brandy

750ml (1¼ pints) lemonade

ice to serve

Sangria

1 Put the lemon, orange and lime slices into a large jug. Add the wine, brandy and lemonade. Stir together to mix well and serve in glasses with plenty of ice.

EASY	NUTRITIONAL INFORMATION		Serves
Preparation Time 5 minutes	**Per Serving** 80 calories, 0g fat, 18g carbohydrate, 0g salt	Vegetarian Gluten free • Dairy free	**8**

250ml (9fl oz) orange juice

150ml (¼ pint) pineapple juice

150ml (¼ pint) freshly squeezed lemon juice

150ml (¼ pint) fruit nectar (mango or peach)

50ml (2fl oz) blackcurrant cordial (such as Ribena)

750ml (1¼ pints) sparkling water

ice cubes

orange slices to serve

Fruit Punch

1 Pour all the fruit juices and blackcurrant cordial into a large pitcher or bowl, stir to mix, then add the sparkling water and a couple of handfuls of ice cubes.

2 Pour the fruit punch into glasses and finish each with a slice of orange.

Serves 8	EASY	NUTRITIONAL INFORMATION	
	Preparation Time 5 minutes	Per Serving 37 calories, trace fat, 9g carbohydrate, 0g salt	Vegetarian Gluten free • Dairy free

Try Something Different

Instead of elderflower cordial, use strawberry cordial or lime and lemongrass cordial.

Elderflower Sparkle

37.5cl bottle elderflower cordial, chilled

6 x 75cl bottles sparkling wine, chilled

1 Up to 30 minutes before serving, pour a splash of cordial into each champagne flute.

2 When ready to serve, fill each glass with sparkling wine.

EASY	NUTRITIONAL INFORMATION		Serves
Preparation Time 10 minutes, plus chilling	**Per Serving** 188 calories, 0g fat, 17g carbohydrate, 0g salt	Vegetarian Gluten free • Dairy free	**20**

Try Something Different

For a less sweet drink, double the amount of juice and top up with sparkling water.

Cranberry Cooler

75ml (3fl oz) cranberry juice

ice cubes

lemonade

slice of lemon (optional)

1 Put the cranberry juice in a tall glass half-filled with ice. Top up with lemonade, mix together quickly and finish with a slice of lemon if you like.

Serves 1	EASY		NUTRITIONAL INFORMATION	
	Preparation Time 2 minutes		**Per Serving** 51 calories, trace fat, 13g carbohydrate, 0g salt	Vegetarian Gluten free • Dairy free

Glossary

Al dente Italian term commonly used to describe foods, especially pasta and vegetables, which are cooked until tender but still firm to the bite.

Baking blind Pre-baking a pastry case before filling. The pastry case is lined with greaseproof paper and weighted down with dried beans or ceramic baking beans.

Baste To spoon the juices and melted fat over meat, poultry, game or vegetables during roasting to keep them moist. The term is also used to describe spooning a marinade over food.

Beat To incorporate air into an ingredient or mixture by agitating it vigorously with a spoon, fork, whisk or electric mixer. The technique is also used to soften ingredients.

Bind To mix beaten egg or other liquid into a dry mixture to hold it together.

Blanch To immerse food briefly in fast-boiling water to loosen skins, such as peaches or tomatoes, or to remove bitterness, or to destroy enzymes and preserve the colour, flavour and texture of vegetables (especially prior to freezing).

Bouquet garni Small bunch of herbs – usually a mixture of parsley stems, thyme and a bay leaf – tied in muslin and used to flavour stocks, soups and stews.

Braise To cook meat, poultry, game or vegetables slowly in a small amount of liquid in a pan or casserole with a tight-fitting lid. The food is usually first browned in oil or fat.

Caramelise To heat sugar or sugar syrup slowly until it is brown in colour; ie forms a caramel.

Chill To cool food in the fridge.

Compote Fresh or dried fruit stewed in sugar syrup. Served hot or cold.

Coulis A smooth fruit or vegetable purée, thinned if necessary to a pouring consistency.

Cream To beat together fat and sugar until the mixture is pale and fluffy, and resembles whipped cream in texture and colour. The method is used in cakes and puddings which contain a high proportion of fat and require the incorporation of a lot of air.

Croûtons Small pieces of fried or toasted bread, served with soups and salads.

Crudités Raw vegetables, usually cut into slices or sticks, typically served with a dipping sauce.

Curdle To cause sauces or creamed mixtures to separate, usually by overheating or over-beating.

Cure To preserve fish, meat or poultry by smoking, drying or salting.

Deglaze To heat stock, wine or other liquid with the cooking juices left in the pan after roasting or sautéeing, scraping and stirring vigorously to dissolve the sediment on the bottom of the pan.

Dice To cut food into small cubes.

Dredge To sprinkle food generously with flour, sugar, icing sugar etc.

Dust To sprinkle lightly with flour, cornflour, icing sugar etc.

Escalope Thin slice of meat, such as pork, veal or turkey, from the top of the leg, usually pan-fried.

Fillet Term used to describe boned breasts of birds, boned sides of fish, and the undercut of a loin of beef, lamb, pork or veal.

Flake To separate food, such as cooked fish, into natural pieces.

Folding in Method of combining a whisked or creamed mixture with other ingredients by cutting and folding so that it retains its lightness. A large metal spoon or plastic-bladed spatula is used.

Fry To cook food in hot fat or oil. There are various methods: shallow-frying in a little fat in a shallow pan; deep-frying where the food is totally immersed in oil; dry-frying in which fatty foods are cooked in a non-stick pan without extra fat; see also Stir-frying.

Garnish A decoration, usually edible, such as parsley or lemon, which is used to enhance the appearance of a savoury dish.

Gluten A protein constituent of grains, such as wheat and rye, which develops when the flour is mixed with water to give the dough elasticity.

Griddle A flat, heavy, metal plate used on the hob for cooking scones or for searing savoury ingredients.

Gut To clean out the entrails from fish.

Hull To remove the stalk and calyx from soft fruits, such as strawberries.

Infuse To immerse flavourings, such as aromatic vegetables, herbs, spices and vanilla, in a liquid to impart flavour. Usually the infused liquid is brought to the boil, then left to stand for a while.

Julienne Fine 'matchstick' strips of vegetables or citrus zest, sometimes used as a garnish.

Macerate To soften and flavour raw or dried foods by soaking in a liquid, eg soaking fruit in alcohol.

Marinate To soak raw meat, poultry or game – usually in a mixture of oil, wine, vinegar and flavourings – to soften and impart flavour. The mixture, which is known as a marinade, may also be used to baste the food during cooking.

Medallion Small round piece of meat, usually beef or veal.

Mince To cut food into very fine pieces, using a mincer, food processor or knife.

Parboil To boil a vegetable or other food for part of its cooking time before finishing it by another method.

Pare To finely peel the skin or zest from vegetables or fruit.

Poach To cook food gently in liquid at simmering point; the surface should be just trembling.

Pot-roast To cook meat in a covered pan with some fat and a little liquid.

Purée To pound, sieve or liquidise vegetables, fish or fruit to a smooth pulp. Purées often form the basis for soups and sauces.

Reduce To fast-boil stock or other liquid in an uncovered pan to evaporate water and concentrate the flavour.

Refresh To cool hot vegetables very quickly by plunging into ice-cold water or holding under cold running water in order to stop the cooking process and preserve the colour.

Roast To cook food by dry heat in the oven.

Roux A mixture of equal quantities of butter (or other fat) and flour cooked together to form the basis of many sauces.

Rubbing in Method of incorporating fat into flour by rubbing between the fingertips, used when a short texture is required. Used for pastry, cakes, scones and biscuits.

Salsa Piquant sauce made from chopped fresh vegetables and sometimes fruit.

Sauté To cook food in a small quantity of fat over a high heat, shaking the pan constantly – usually in a sauté pan (a frying pan with straight sides and a wide base).

Scald To pour boiling water over food to clean it, or loosen skin, eg tomatoes. Also used to describe heating milk to just below boiling point.

Score To cut parallel lines in the surface of food, such as fish (or the fat layer on meat), to improve its appearance or help it cook more quickly.

Sear To brown meat quickly in a little hot fat before grilling or roasting.

Seasoned flour Flour mixed with a little salt and pepper, used for dusting meat, fish etc., before frying.

Shred To grate cheese or slice vegetables into very fine pieces or strips.

Sieve To press food through a perforated sieve to obtain a smooth texture.

Sift To shake dry ingredients through a sieve to remove lumps.

Simmer To keep a liquid just below boiling point.

Skim To remove froth, scum or fat from the surface of stock, gravy, stews, jam etc. Use either a skimmer, a spoon or kitchen paper.

Steam To cook food in steam, usually in a steamer over rapidly boiling water.

Steep To immerse food in warm or cold liquid to soften it, and sometimes to draw out strong flavours.

Stew To cook food, such as tougher cuts of meat, in flavoured liquid which is kept at simmering point.

Stir-fry To cook small, even-sized pieces of food rapidly in a little fat, tossing constantly over a high heat.

Sweat To cook chopped or sliced vegetables in a little fat without liquid in a covered pan over a low heat to soften.

Tepid The term used to describe temperature of approximately blood heat, ie 37°C (98.7°F).

Vanilla sugar Sugar in which a vanilla pod has been stored to impart its flavour.

Whipping (whisking) Beating air rapidly into a mixture either with a manual or electric whisk. Whipping usually refers to cream.

Zest The thin, coloured outer layer of citrus fruit, which can be removed in fine strips with a zester.

Index